Criminal Justice
Recent Scholarship

Edited by
Nicholas P. Lovrich

A Series from LFB Scholarly

White Collar Crime in Housing
Mortgage Fraud in the United States

Cynthia Koller

LFB Scholarly Publishing LLC
El Paso 2012

Library of Congress Cataloging-in-Publication Data

Koller, Cynthia, 1960-
White collar crime in housing : mortgage fraud in the United States / Cynthia Koller.
p. cm. -- (Criminal justice : recent scholarship)
Includes bibliographical references and index.
ISBN 978-1-59332-534-3 (hardcover : alk. paper)
1. Mortgage loans--Corrupt practices--United States. 2. Subprime mortgage
loans--Corrupt practices--United States. 3. Housing--United States. 4. White collar crimes--United States. I. Title.
HG2040.5.U5K65 2012
364.16'8--dc23

2012017594

ISBN 978-1-59332-534-3

Printed on acid-free 250-year-life paper.

Manufactured in the United States of America.

Table of Contents

List of Tables

List of Figures

CHAPTER 1

White Collar Crime in Housing

> Despite the strong support the economic system provides for the ideals of competitive individualism, it is clear that the pursuit of economic self-interest must be contained within some normative boundaries – or social and economic chaos would be the ultimate result. The economic rationality necessary to industrialism demands that exchange relationships be based on some set of mutually accepted standards. Without these rules, exchange relationships would become vastly more difficult for all parties involved, and many of the complex economic relationships characteristic of modern society would be virtually impossible to maintain (Coleman, 1987:421).

Statement of the Problem

Headlines of record home foreclosures, financial institution bankruptcies, and white collar crime indictments have littered the news media on a daily basis over the past few years. A breakdown in "exchange relationship" standards in the form of financial crimes have assuredly contributed to this unprecedented display of economic self-*destruction*, and contributed to the economic crisis which continues to reverberate around the world. By the close of the first decade in the new millennium, the Federal Bureau of Investigation (FBI) reported that annual losses due to fraud in the mortgage market alone had been estimated at $4 to $6 billion, and the problem continued to escalate

(FBI, 2010). By 2012, these estimates rose to over $10 billion in annual losses (FBI, 2012). FBI (2011:13) data indicates that of the total number of Suspicious Activity Reports[1] received, those associated with mortgage fraud doubled between 2008 and 2009, with 70,533 received in 2010 alone; this represented an increase of 5% from 2009 and 11% from 2008 filings. As of the end of 2011, there were 2.590 pending mortgage fraud investigations, of which 70% involved losses exceeding $1 million (FBI, 2012).

The United States Securities and Exchange Commission (SEC) workload has also dramatically increased over the past few years as criminal and civil mortgage fraud and related enforcement actions have similarly soared (SEC, 2012). These record volumes are expected to continue rising as individuals, organizations, and regulators continue to struggle in pursuit of economic equilibrium and a return to some semblance of economic rationality and fiscal accountability. Other factors are certainly at play with respect to the crisis in the mortgage market (e.g., inflated housing prices, weakening of the U.S. dollar), yet frauds (e.g., material misrepresentations, erroneous bundling and securitizing of uncollateralized debt) have compromised the normative boundaries of the mortgage system, have contributed to the financial chaos, and have tainted a potentially valid and fruitful avenue for home ownership in the United States.

Along with mortgage fraud, white collar crime in the form of antitrust violations, fraudulent bankruptcy, corporate practice, securities transactions, health care and insurance claims, and the like ranked as

---

[1] Federal law requires SARs to be submitted to FinCEN by financial businesses which encounter incidents of suspected money laundering or fraud (Internal Revenue Service, 2010). The IRS explains that a suspicious transaction requires a financial institution, such as a Money Service Business (MSB), to "file a SAR when it knows or suspects that: the funds come from illegal activity or disguise funds from illegal activity; the transaction is structured to evade BSA requirements or appears to serve no known business or apparent lawful purpose; or, the MSB is being used to facilitate criminal activity."

the number seven investigative priority of the FBI at the close of the last decade (FBI, 2010). With public corruption ranked as its number four priority, the FBI substantiated that crime "in the suites" represents a vital concern to the nation's top law enforcement officials. White collar crime (the criminal event) and white collar criminality (criminal behavior) also represent a vital concern to criminologists, who continue to examine the intricacies of this particular form of offending and how to better regulate and deter it (Benson, Madensen, & Eck, 2009). As Benson and colleagues point out, however, before specific white collar crimes can be prevented or controlled, the opportunity structures and processes defining and precipitating these offenses must first be examined and understood.

The literature regarding the role of opportunity in the etiology, prevention, and control of crime "in the streets" has been plentiful over the past few decades (see e.g., Cohen & Felson, 1979; Cornish & Clarke, 2003; Eck & Clarke, 2003; Weisburd, Wyckoff, Ready, et al., 2006). However, theoretical developments with respect to white collar crime opportunity structures have been slower to develop (Shapiro, 1990; Beken & Balcaen, 2006; Benson & Simpson, 2009), and to date no clear theoretical or methodological perspective has received widespread interest or support. To be sure, attention has been given to the opportunity structure of white collar crimes in general (Coleman, 1987; Benson et al., 2009; Benson & Simpson, 2009), small business crime (Barlow, 1993), and to specific crimes such as fraud in the savings and loan industry (Pontell & Calavita, 1990). Yet even these analyses fall short in identifying the principal mechanisms, or demonstrating the processes, by which crime spreads within an industry.

Sutherland (1983:246) argued that the diffusion of illegal practices helps to explain how and why criminal techniques and definitions are learned, accepted, and spread. He similarly failed to elaborate on the "diffusion" process itself, however, indicating rather that businessmen engage in crime when they are able to modify legitimate business practices into illegitimate means in the pursuit of personal and organizational benefits. This is consistent with Sutherland's definition of white collar crime, and supports his implication that the reinvention of legal business innovations into illegal practices may occur as regularly as the spread of legal and illegal innovations themselves. This being said, Sutherland understood that irrespective of the original legality of an opportunity, there could be no criminal event without exposure to, and adoption of, crime-favorable motivations, as well as access to the opportunity itself.

In sum, the concept of white collar crime, as distinct from other property or violent crimes, has weathered countless definitional, theoretical, and empirical challenges throughout the decades since the concept was first articulated by Sutherland in the late 1930s (see e.g., Hirschi & Gottfredson, 1987; Tittle, Burke & Jackson, 1986). Although progress continues to be made with respect to understanding *who* commits these offenses, *how* they do so, and *why*, the underlying opportunity structures and processes which stimulate and facilitate these offenses have yet to be fully elucidated (Benson et al., 2009).

Overview of Current Study/Research Questions

The purpose of this study is to contribute to the field's understanding of white collar crime opportunity structures by investigating how and why legal and illegal practices spread throughout the mortgage industry over time, and how this can best be examined through the diffusion of innovations framework (Rogers, 2003) and a qualitative assessment of mortgage industry practitioner perspectives. More specifically, this study: (1) utilizes diffusion theory to interpret the growing incidence and prevalence of lending and fraud in the subprime mortgage market (see Utt, 2008); and, (2) utilizes interviews to capture insider views on the subprime opportunity structure and the benefits/problems it posed for the industry. It is anticipated that the specific applicability of diffusion theory to the study of white collar crime, and more generally to the study of other areas of concern to criminologists, will be illuminated through this inquiry. The following research questions were developed to facilitate the investigation:

1. What has been the rate and extent of the diffusion of subprime lending, and has this diffusion been consistent with the S-curve distribution notable in the classic diffusion model (Rogers, 2003)?

2. What has been the rate and extent of the diffusion of fraud in the subprime market?

3. Do knowledge of financial innovations and their potential reinventions (legal or illegal) diffuse simultaneously, or is there a lag between the innovation and the reinvention diffusions?

4. Why and how was the subprime mortgage originally devised and presented to the financial community (e.g., with respect to need, source and communication channels) and what is the opportunity structure for this innovation (i.e., who can use it)?

5. What specific characteristics of the subprime lending innovation contributed to its rate and extent of adoption, and what characteristics contributed to fraud in the market due to its diffusion and its reinvention?

6. What communication channels (e.g., formal or informal) have been most likely to diffuse legitimate as compared to illegitimate applications of the innovation?

7. Are there characteristics of the subprime loan and lending process which made it more likely to be reinvented for fraudulent purposes than other mortgage tools and techniques (e.g., prime loans)?

8. What types of regulatory controls could have been included in the original innovation or its diffusion (innovation-decision) process to minimize the risk of its use for illegal gains?

The combination of the ideological perspectives of diffusion theory and criminological theories represented in these questions makes them well-suited to the investigation; these perspectives are more fully elaborated on in Chapters 3 and 4.

Diffusion is defined as the "process in which an innovation is communicated through certain channels over time among the members of a social system" (Rogers, 2003:5). Rogers notes that the spread of an innovation can be planned or spontaneous, and the innovation itself can take any material, process, or ideological form – for example, from hybrid corn planting to prescription drug use (Strang & Soule, 1998). The diffusion of innovations research is plentiful and continues to grow. Rogers (2003) reports that a variety of disciplines have utilized the theory over the past fifty years, including anthropology, sociology (early, rural, public health and medical, and general), education, communication, marketing and management, and geography.

Similar to investigations of offender characteristics by criminologists, the characteristics of innovation adopters (i.e., innovators, early adopters, early majority, late majority and laggards) appear to be the most frequent area of historical research interest across these various disciplines (Rogers, 2003). Yet as many authors note, all structural, cultural, and interpersonal aspects of the diffusion process (e.g., characteristics of innovations, communication channels, rate of adoption, reinvention) present empirical opportunities. For example, related to criminal justice/criminology issues, diffusion theory has been used to examine school district adoptions of Drug Abuse and Resistance Education (DARE) programs (Rogers, 1993, as cited in Rogers, 2003), the spread of check forgery (Lacoste & Tremblay, 2003), state death penalty law adoption (Mooney & Lee, 1999), intermediate fraud among investors in a gas and oil business (Baker & Faulkner, 2003), and police organization innovativeness (King, 2000; Weiss, 1997). In combination, these few studies (reviewed in Chapter 5) exemplify how legitimate or viable opportunities are subject to distortion by individuals and organizations during the innovation-decision and adoption process through what is referred to as reinvention (Rogers, 2003) which is, by definition, a fundamental element of white collar crime.

In conclusion, the recent spread of the subprime mortgage innovation, and the fraud that has accompanied it, provides a relevant challenge for criminology to more thoroughly enter and contribute to the diffusion research tradition. It also provides a significant occasion to further assess the viability of diffusion of innovations theory[2] to criminological research. At the risk of supplying simply one more typology of crime (subprime mortgage fraud), this project makes a valuable contribution to the opportunity perspective of white collar crime (see Benson et al., 2009; Benson & Simpson, 2009). This contribution is accomplished by examining subprime mortgage practitioners' perspectives on how a legitimate business innovation was originally structured and diffused, how and why illegitimate reinventions of the tool occurred, and what can be done to potentially limit this latter phenomenon through the implementation of controls or effective oversight institutions in the diffusion process.

Organization of the Study

In demonstrating how the diffusion and reinvention of innovations form and transpire, the ways in which business practitioners perceive and create (or take advantage of) opportunities can begin to be illuminated. To accomplish this end, this study has been organized as follows: Chapter 2 provides a fundamental explanation of how the mortgage industry in the U.S. is structured and operates, and how innovative subprime lending became an integral component of residential real estate purchasing, financing, and investing throughout the 1990s. This chapter also details the ineffectiveness of the financial system to properly manage the risk associated with this type of unconventional mortgage lending, and how this, along with a variety of

[2] Diffusion of innovation, diffusion of innovations, and diffusion theory are used interchangeably throughout this monograph.

other factors, including fraud (e.g., material misrepresentations of assets, income, etc.), contributed to the height of the subprime crisis in 2007. Finally, this segment introduces the notion that much of the motivation and opportunity for partaking in mortgage fraud is structured within the range of legitimate activities in which individual and corporate participants engage, and estimates of the extent of fraud are provided.

Chapter 3 reviews of some of the more pertinent criminological theories that have been applied to white collar crime. The objective of the discussion is to provide a general overview of white collar crime theorizing and to demonstrate the viability of existing criminological theory to explain white collar offenders and their motivations, and, white collar offenses and their opportunity structures. In addition to highlighting the contributions of Sutherland (1940), the theoretical clarifications and extensions made by many others over the years with respect to opportunity, associations, and routines are also reviewed to illustrate how far the field has advanced in its understanding of how specific factors influence crime.

Chapter 4 provides an introductory review of diffusion of innovations theory. Chapter 5 explains how utilizing the diffusion of innovations framework to interpret subprime mortgage innovation and fraud can extend criminological theory in explaining white collar crime opportunities and white collar criminality.

Chapter 6 addresses the methodology of this project, including an argument for a qualitative approach to studying practitioner perceptions and white collar crime opportunities, as well as a review of the sampling and data collection utilized. The results are reported in Chapters 7 and 8 which address each of the research questions in turn, and provide insights from the interview participants to help understand the issues from the perspectives of the practitioners in the field. It is demonstrated that these mortgage/real estate professionals, who had a diversity of education, experience, qualifications, and job responsibilities, possessed quite similar opinions about what transpired with the subprime innovation over time. It is also illustrated that despite their differences in background and roles in the mortgage system, their interpretations of historical events and of the structure and operations of the housing and financial industries are surprisingly consistent. And finally, it is shown that even with these similar perceptions, each participant offered a unique perspective on the research questions and provided rich forms of information that helped address the questions and issues from a variety of angles.

A discussion of the results (as viewed through five primary innovation characteristics) and of the applicability of criminological and diffusion theories to the study of subprime mortgage fraud and white collar crime are provided in Chapter 9. Elements of various criminological theories are identified and noted as being evident in the qualitative accounts of the mortgage industry practitioners. It is demonstrated that the perceived characteristics of subprime lending, as well as the attributes of subprime mortgage reinvention, or subprime fraud, are discernible from the interview transcripts. These attributes of the subprime opportunity are also shown to be consistent with those noted in classic diffusion theory, and include relative advantage, compatibility, complexity, trialability, and observability. Chapter 10 completes the study with a reiteration of the theoretical arguments linking diffusion theory to the study and understanding of white collar crime motivation and opportunities, and includes a note on directions for further research.

CHAPTER2

Subprime Mortgaging and Fraud

The United States Mortgage Industry

Historical mortgage lending in the United States (U.S.) occurred almost exclusively at the local level, with all parties involved in the transaction (i.e., borrowers and lenders) working and residing in the same communities. Buyers/borrowers knew their bankers and the lenders knew their customers; the bank would lend the money from its own coffers and the borrower would repay the bank. In this type of exchange relationship, or when "benefits are given with the expectation of receiving a comparable benefit in return or as repayment for a benefit received previously" (Clark & Mills, 1993:684), the participants in the transaction share a long-term mutual interest in the quality of the relationship and the performance of the "benefit" – or, in this case, the mortgage loan. Under this scenario, as Stiglitz (2008) notes, banks had a greater financial incentive to screen loan applicants when they retained the mortgages. As such, this type of localized and highly regulated liaison encouraged responsible risk management and customer service, and non-qualified borrowers were not an issue as they had no ability to enter into this type of relationship (Bitner, 2008).

As financial markets grew to keep pace with record consumer and investor demands in the latter part of the 20th century, however, the mortgage financing industry also experienced unprecedented change and growth. By the early 1980s, certain events had begun to unfold, altering the structure of the mortgage market and opening the financing door to many under-qualified loan-seekers (see below). By the mid-

1990s, homeownership started to become a reality for a larger segment of the population through the subprime mortgage, primarily due to the growth in mortgage lending by newly developed subprime lending firms as well as by existing financial institutions (Chomsisengphet & Pennington-Cross, 2006; Immergluck & Smith, 2005).

Subprime Defined

The term "subprime" has no distinct or universal definition. The *Oxford English Dictionary* (2008) explains that the concept historically referred to loans having preferential terms, but this is no longer the case.[3] Subprime is now understood to reflect the credit status of the *borrower* (e.g., credit challenged), the conditions of the *loan* (e.g., higher interest rates and fees), or the characteristics of the *lender* (e.g., institutions which specialize in subprime loans). Lending institutions have their own determination of what borrower and loan characteristics qualify the parties and/or transaction as "subprime" based on how the transaction fits into their own portfolios or the portfolios of their secondary-market buyers and investors. For purposes of this study the term subprime should be considered within the context of the present setting – for example, referring to *high-risk* borrowers, loans, or lenders.

---

[3] "The term *subprime* has become all too familiar as a result of the current credit crisis, which is attributed in part to the proliferation of subprime loans – loans made on unfavourable terms to borrowers unable to qualify for conventional loans. While researching the term, *OED* editors were surprised to discover an earlier financial sense, with quite the opposite meaning. The familiar current sense is attested only from 1993, but as early as 1976, *subprime* was being used to describe an especially desirable type of loan, one which charged less than the **prime rate of interest** and was offered only to the most reliable commercial borrowers. That meaning is now rare, and in the new sense which has replaced it, it is not the interest rate of the loan which is "less than prime," but the rating of the borrowers themselves" (*Oxford English Dictionary*, 2008).

Subprime Lending

Three particular legislative actions have been credited with stimulating the birth of the subprime industry. These federal statutes included the Depository Institutions Deregulation and Money Control Act of 1980 (DIDMCA), the Alternative Mortgage Transaction Parity Act of 1982, and the Tax Reform Act of 1986 (Bitner, 2008; Chomsisengphet & Pennington-Cross, 2006). Taken in combination, these events essentially created the subprime business as it enabled lenders to begin charging higher interest rates and fees (exceeding state limits), to offer adjustable interest rate mortgages (ARMs) and balloon payment options, and allowed individuals to begin taking home mortgage interest tax deductions. Although other changes preceded these Acts in the late 1960s through the 1970s, such as the Fair Housing Act of 1968, Equal Credit Opportunity Act of 1974, Home Mortgage Disclosure Act of 1975, and the Community Reinvestment Act of 1977, Bitner notes it was not until the enactment of the DIDMCA that the business of subprime lending became a "legal" enterprise.

In addition to the legislative activity that positioned previously or otherwise under-qualified or credit-challenged borrowers to enter into exchange relationships with lenders, market changes also "contributed to the growth and maturation of subprime loans" (Chomsisengphet & Pennington-Cross, 2006:38). Brokerage and securitization were key elements in this growth (and in the industry's segmentation), as it gave traditional and non-traditional (non-depository) lenders the ability to supply and deliver creative financing and credit, while simultaneously passing on its accompanying risk.

Figure 2.1 illustrates the general mortgage process as it is understood to most recently exist in the U.S. As depicted, the industry has seen considerable change since the days of localized lending. The federal government played a critical role in the modifications to this industry by enabling and encouraging securitization and off-balance sheet lending (pass through financing), particularly through the passage of the Financial Institutions Reform, Recovery, and Enforcement Act of 1989 (Aalbers, 2009). This Act, adopted in the wake of the savings and

Figure 2.1 The Subprime Mortgage System

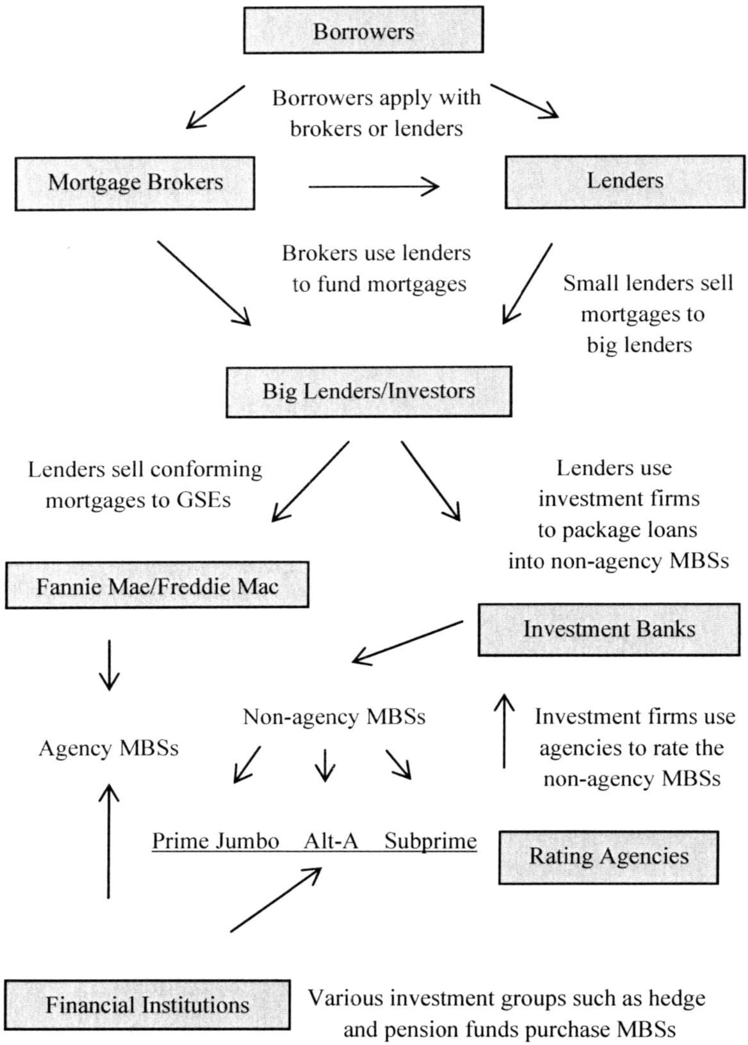

*FHA and VA loans excluded. Adapted from Bitner (2008:28)

loan crisis, attended to bank lending and appraisal regulation, but also encouraged the Government Sponsored Enterprises (GSEs) to facilitate lending opportunities to low- and moderate-income individuals. With most new subprime mortgage lenders operating as non-banks, however, these regulations may have proven to be more ideal than real.

As illustrated in Figure 2.1, subprime loans find their way into investment and pension fund portfolios in the form of Mortgage-Backed Securities (MBSs).[4] This "food chain," as Bitner (2008) refers to it, also illustrates that the business of mortgage lending plays a crucial role in the financial health and stability of the overall economy. As will be demonstrated later, problems in one area may have repercussions throughout the entire system.

In sum, contemporary subprime lending is a relatively recent innovation. It facilitates a higher interest rate, higher fee market

---

[4] "Mortgage-backed securities are "pass through" securities where the initial lender still services the mortgages; the lender collects fees and then passes through interest and principal to owners of the bundled mortgages" (Glaeser & Kallal, 1997:68). Glaeser and Kallal explain that the main issuers of conforming MBSs are the GSEs, who bundle these products for sale to dealers (such as Salomon Brothers and Bear Sterns) for resale to pension and mutual funds. As noted in Figure 2.1, non-conforming loans also proceed through the bundling and securitization process, but not through the insured GSEs. Heuson, Passmore, and Sparks (2001:337) explain that in the secondary market of MBSs "a monopolist sells mortgage-backed securities, which yield a liquidity benefit, in exchange for mortgages offered by originators. The monopolist/securitizer sets both the price for these mortgages and the credit-quality standard that qualifies a mortgage for purchase. Although credit scoring ensures that originators do not enjoy an information advantage over the securitizer, they do enjoy a "first mover advantage" in selecting which qualifying mortgages to sell." This ultimately contributes to "asymmetrical risk" (Chen, Liao, & Yang, 2008; Hildebrand, 2008) and influences mortgage credit availability and mortgage interest rates.

product than the conventional or prime loan, and it was originally devised to promote homeownership for those who would not have traditionally qualified for financing. Yet the innovation has had its share of concerned analysts who have substantiated the claim that subprime lending enveloped many prime customers over the years as well (Aalbers, 2009; Bitner, 2008; Courchane, Surette, & Zorn, 2004; Foote, Gerardi, Goette, & Witten, 2008; Lander, Barker, Zabelina, & Williams, 2009). For example, Aalbers (2009:95) argues that "subprime lending should not be defined as lending to borrowers with poor credit, but as lending at higher fees and interest rates whether or not borrowers actually have bad credit." Lander et al. (2009) agree, defining this as "predatory lending" or the offering of subprime loans to individuals who qualify for prime loans, as some borrowers are subjected to higher costs for reasons other than credit risk (Courchane et al., 2004).[5]

Aalbers explains this should come as no surprise:

> Selling subprime loans to prime borrowers was good business for both mortgage lenders and brokers. Lenders could charge higher interest rates on subprime loans and thus make more money. For this reason lenders gave brokers bigger sales fees for selling subprime loans. Brokers did not have negative results as a consequence of defaulting borrowers, as they only get paid for what they sell. And defaulting borrowers actually created a bigger market for refinancing, which implied that brokers could make more money on clients by selling them another loan (Aalbers, 2009:95-96).

Furthermore, Foote and colleagues (2008:292) concur, noting their review of Massachusetts' 1990s lending data revealed "persons with

---

[5] Chomsisengphet and Pennington-Cross (2006:31) explain: "Borrower cost associated with subprime lending is driven primarily by two factors: credit history and down payment requirements. This contrasts with the prime market, where borrower cost is primarily driven by the down payment alone, given that minimum credit history requirements are satisfied."

high credit scores were increasingly likely to take out subprime loans." These authors also claim, however, that despite higher credit scores, these same borrowers may not have qualified for loans with prime lenders anyway due to high "loan-to-value (LTV) or debt-to-income (DTI) ratios, or they lacked full documentation of borrower income and assets" (p. 292).[6]

Regardless of how one defines subprime lending (see above), the process is correlated with risk, as lenders can only rationally tolerate the increased risk these credit- and/or collateral-challenged borrowers may present by collecting higher interest rates and fees (Calem, Gillen, & Wachter, 2004). In fact, the management of risk goes to the heart of subprime lending, yet along with fraudulent practices, its eventual mismanagement arguably helped to facilitate the demise of the subprime lending industry. Before discussing how risk management became problematic, an overview of the growth of the subprime industry will put the breadth and depth of this task into perspective.

Market Growth

During the 1970s-1980s, legislative, regulatory, economic, and industry events began to shape what would eventually become the "subprime mortgage market." Legislation and regulation paved the way for new product and process development, and with the encouragement of the federal government, the financial industry welcomed this new form of potentially profitable lending. It was not until the mid-1990s, however, that the growth in subprime lending started to truly become established and to increase (Bitner, 2008; Chomsisengphet & Pennington-Cross,

---

[6] Smith (2007:2) also notes subprime borrower characteristics include individuals with "recent delinquencies, foreclosures, judgments, bankruptcies and comparably high debt to service ratios" and that subprime lending expanded to include loans to middle-class borrowers whose loans were not appropriate for sale in the primary market.

Table 2.1: Subprime Growth

Year	Total Subprime Originations (billions)	Top 25 Subprime Originations (billions)	Top 25 Market Share of Subprime	Total Originations (billions)	Subprime Market Share of Total
1995	$65.0	$25.5	39.3%	$639.4	10.2%
1996	$96.8	$45.3	46.8%	$785.3	12.3%
1997	$124.5	$75.1	60.3%	$859.1	14.5%
1998	$150.0	$94.3	62.9%	$1450.0	10.3%
1999	$160.0	$105.6	66.0%	$1310.0	12.2%
2000	$138.0	$102.2	74.1%	$1048.0	13.2%
2001	$173.3	$126.8	73.2%	$2058.0	8.4%
2002	$213.0	$187.6	88.1%	$2680.0	7.9%
2003	$332.0	$310.1	93.4%	$3760.0	8.8%

"Individual firm data are from *Inside B&C Lending* and are generally based on security issuance or previously reported data" (*Inside B&C Lending* as cited in Chomsisengphet and Pennington-Cross, 2006:37).

2006; Foote et al., 2008). This growth has also been attributed to fluctuating interest rates, declining loan originations in the prime market, and as stated previously, the industry's ability to bundle and securitize subprime loans into MBSs.

The growth was further facilitated on the supply side by the entrance of countless new non-depository finance companies – for example, mortgage brokerages (Chomsisengphet & Pennington-Cross; Immergluck & Smith, 2005). Table 2.1 illustrates the growth in subprime originations from 1995 through 2003. Chomsisengphet and Pennington-Cross explain the total market share of subprime lending originally peaked in 1997 and leveled off for a few years due to more extensive prime loan refinancing (in response to falling interest rates as well as a number of securitization and global economic concerns). Also note the market share of the top 25 mortgage lenders as shown in Table 2.1; their share of subprime originations grew from 39.3% in 1995 to 93.4% by 2003 (which reflects the uneven distribution of risk within the financial markets; see below).

Table 2.2: Securitization Rate* by Loan Type

Year	FHA/VA	Conventional	Subprime
1995	101.1	45.6	28.4
1996	98.1	52.5	39.5
1997	100.7	45.9	53.0
1998	102.3	62.2	55.1
1999	88.1	67.0	37.4
2000	89.5	55.6	40.4
2001	102.5	71.5	54.7
2002	92.6	72.8	57.6
2003	84.9	75.9	58.7

Source: *Inside MBS & ABS* as cited in Chomsisengphet and Pennington-Cross (2006:38); "NOTE: Subprime securities include both MBS and ABS backed by subprime loans."

*Securitization rate = dollars securitized divided by dollars originated.

Another indication of the substantial short-term growth in the subprime industry is clearly evidenced by the volume of subprime loans bundled into securities (see Table 2.2; Note: MBSs can include asset-backed securities, and may be referred to as ABSs). Immergluck and Smith (2005:365) further claim that outstanding ABSs "tripled from $33 billion in 1995 to $90 billion [in] 1997 and grew to $286 billion by May 2002, for an annual growth rate of 36%" with most of the funding of these securities coming from subprime lending. Pavlov estimates outstanding MBSs approached $1.7 trillion by 1997, and "encompassed nearly half of all outstanding United States' mortgage loans" (2001:185).

Growth continued to move in an upward direction from 1995 forward, with subprime lending making up less than 1% of the market share in the early 1990s, peaking in 1997 at 14.5% and dropping to 8.4% by 2001 (Chomsisengphet & Pennington-Cross, 2006). Chomsisengphet and Pennington-Cross also report that between 2002 and 2003, subprime originations increased another 56-62%. Although it is obvious that Immergluck and Smith (2005), Pavlov (2001), and Chomsisengphet and Pennington-Cross have used different data sources and vary in their estimates, one thing is certain: the subprime product enjoyed virtual overnight popularity and quickly became a major component of not only the U.S. financial structure, but by MBS extension, the global economy as well.

Furthermore, during the 1990s, the number of new independent mortgage brokers increased 14% annually. By the year 2000, "30,000 mortgage brokerage firms employed an estimated 240,000 workers and accounted for approximately 55% of all mortgage originations" (Immergluck & Smith, 2005:365). Key here is that mortgages originated by brokers are *twice* as likely to be subprime than those originated by lenders (Immergluck & Smith).

The growth of subprime lending in the 1990s was attributable to a variety of market and industry factors. These include, but are not limited to: consumer demand; rising interest rates; declining loan originations in the prime market; the bundling and securitizing of subprime loans into MBSs; and, the number of new non-depository finance companies (e.g., mortgage brokerage firms). Despite the benefits of this growth to potential homebuyers and the other participants in the mortgage industry process, however, change on this scale is typically accompanied by unintended consequences. Hildebrand (2008) argues this rapid expansion (of the U.S. housing market) and the manner in which the industry developed was "clearly excessive" and problematic. It will be shown below that it is more than likely that the rapid infusion of these new demands, products, and players into a traditionally risk-based industry may have undermined the system's ability to foresee or manage that risk.

Risk Assessment and Management

Similar to consumer lending in general (e.g., automobiles, recreational vehicles, unsecured lines-of-credit, etc.), mortgage lending is an inherently risky business. The fundamental risk in both of these types of lending is that when borrowers default on their payments, the lender generally must work with the borrower to restructure the loan, write off the loss, or repossess the property and dispose of it, also usually at a loss. The loan application process is designed to assess original creditworthiness (via credit scores, LTV, DTI; see above) and helps lenders determine the structure and terms of the loan (e.g., collateralized or unsecure, interest rate, down payment, etc.). However, with the eventual advent of stated income, no income verification, no documentation, and no down payment mortgage type lending options and procedures (see below), subprime lending diverged from this traditional financing protocol and evolved into a distinctly unknown and high-risk endeavor (Bitner, 2008).

Due to the evolving structure of the mortgage lending system (e.g., pass-through financing, broker originations) and the securitization process, risks developed in home financing which were not of concern in the general consumer lending arena. For example, as Archer, Ling, and McGill (2003:112) explain, a "significant determinant of the performance of residential mortgage loan portfolios is the rate at which loans are prepaid or refinanced by borrowers." Along with default for non-payment then, the early termination of loans through pay-off or refinancing present substantial risk to the value of MBSs (Pavlov,

2001).[7] As such, regardless of the default risk assessment at the time of the loan application and approval, new types of risk emerge as a loan ages and moves up the mortgage process food chain.

When prepayment becomes another termination risk (besides default), it is easier to understand that when coupled with the segmented structure of this process, the competing demands of its participants, and the overall lack of transparency and asymmetry of information, managing or compensating for this risk of early termination becomes monumental. The sheer number of participants affected by the termination alone is astounding. For example, in the following scenario, the involved parties include the borrower, lender, securitizer (GSE or investment bank) and financial institution:

> MBS securities rise and fall in value based on the exercise of homeowners' prepayment options. When a homeowner prepays a mortgage, the MBS backed by the mortgage is called back at par. Depending on the interest rate environment, prepayment can either hurt or benefit the MBS investor. Thus, for an investor who specializes in the MBS market, prepayment risk represents a risk to the value of his portfolio (Gabaix, Krishnamurthy & Vigneron, 2007:558)

Once again, this is a far cry from the traditional localized mortgage lending scheme and how consumer lending generally continues to operate.

It is important to note that the growth in subprime lending was not simply due to original home purchasing. Similar to the prime market, much of the volume in the subprime market, especially in the late-1990s when housing values climbed and interest rates dropped, came from cash-out and no cash-out refinancing loans. This refinancing enabled borrowers to capitalize on the increased (albeit inflated) equity

---

[7] "Homeowners can substantially impact the holders of these securities by exercising their right to prepay or default. If an investor buys a security well above (or below) par, an unanticipated return of principal can result in a substantial loss (or gain)" (Pavlov, 2001:185).

of their homes for cash in their pockets or more favorable loan structures. Chomsisengphet and Pennington-Cross (2006) report that in the late-1990s, over 50% of subprime originations were for cash-out refinancing, with just over 33% for home purchases. This trend reversed by 2003 as default and interest rates began to climb, with subprime home purchases outnumbering cash-out and no cash-out loans combined, suggesting that although lenders are not risk-aversive, they are at least arguably somewhat risk-sensitive. Still, refinancing is a form of prepayment and represents an early termination risk to the securitized debt that is being processed and held by the upper echelons of the food chain.

The rating agencies, most notably Standard and Poor's (S&P), Moody's, and Fitch, play a key function in the management of risk in the subprime industry (Bitner, 2008). In simple terms, these companies rate the value and risk of MBSs and other items for investment banks, as compared to credit rating agencies (i.e., TransUnion, Experian, and Equifax) who rate individual consumer risk. As displayed in Figure 2.1, the lenders who initially fund mortgages pass these loans onto the GSEs or larger investment banks and firms who package the loans into MBSs which receive a credit-quality standard (e.g., AAA, AA to B, and Equity). The rating determines the value of the bundled pool of mortgages with the intention of having potential purchasers (investors) being informed about the risk level of the product. Yet the securities frequently get spliced into separate investment products, so eventually the "original mortgages are no longer recognizable, [and] judging the quality of the assets is next to impossible" (Bitner, p. 109).

Although rating agencies were, in theory, developed to remain objective and neutral, in many situations they do not have the requisite information to make quality ratings, and they appear to operate at the whim of whoever is paying their fees. The investment banks contract with these rating agencies for the service, and the cost is related to the size of the securities being rated (volume driven), which presents an inherent conflict of interest as noted by Lander and colleagues (2009), when the seller, and not the buyer, pays for the appraisal. Moreover, "while lenders and investment firms have at least some financial interest in the performance of a product, the agencies always get their cut ... even if they drastically misrepresent how a security should perform, they face no liability" (Bitner, 2008:113).

As illuminated herein, from the initial borrower to final investors, financial risk is not evenly distributed throughout the subprime mortgage chain, and this contributed to a host of market and participant behaviors which many believe have contributed to the market collapse. As Hildebrand (2008) contends, the meltdown of the subprime market was predictable and inevitable: with the lack of information transparency in the process, and its asymmetrical structure (profits retained by some and losses borne by others), the system promoted short-sighted, risky behavior and was never truly sustainable (see also Coleman, 1987; Stiglitz, 2008).

Subprime Mortgage Crisis

By the early 2000s, continued expansion of the subprime market appeared limitless as demand for U.S. MBSs began to multiply around the world. Lander et al. (2009) explain that by the end of 2006, nearly 20% of MBSs (agency and non-agency issued; and unregulated mortgage securities) were funded by foreign investors, up from 6% in 1994. For example, Lander and colleagues report that in mid-2006, "China held approximately $108 billion in MBSs, up substantially from $3 billion in 2003 and $100 million in 2002" (p. 8). Although this infusion of capital into the U.S. economy helped stimulate lower interest rates, increased home prices, and higher sales volumes, it also provided a seemingly infinite source of mortgage funds. Nonetheless, for reasons to be discussed below, the mortgage industry "house of cards" came tumbling down by mid-2007, with China and others folding quickly as risk became reality.

A variety of factors led to the subprime crisis, which continues to be manifested in record mortgage defaults and foreclosures, reduced housing values, and record business exits and bankruptcies (Demyanyk, 2009). Demyanyk contends the crisis resulted due to a combination of interest rate resets (maturity of ARMs), fraud, poor underwriting of subprime loans (inattention to risk), the temporary nature of subprime loans, discrimination, a housing market slowdown, and an overall deterioration of loan quality. These factors eventually created a financial emergency that could no longer be ignored by even the most casual observer.

Hildebrand (2008) notes that in July of 2007, S&P announced a downgrade of billions of dollars' worth of subprime debt and was restructuring how it rated MBSs to compensate for poor performance and enlightened risk assessment and management needs. Barr (2007) also reported that Moody's followed suit, with both downgrading hundreds of classes of MBSs due to "unprecedented levels of misrepresentation and fraud, combined with potentially shoddy initial loan data" as well as deteriorating property values and lower fixed-rate loan teaser rates. Albeit mostly in hindsight, many believe that the factors precipitating this crisis were not only inevitable, but should have been anticipated and ultimately prevented (Davis & Karim, 2008; Hildebrand, 2008; Stiglitz, 2008).

In agreement with Stiglitz (2008) that the subprime crisis was predictable, and drawing from Davis' earlier work, Davis and Karim (2008:44) argue there are generic patterns evident prior to most financial crises such as this. These include:

1. Regime shifts, first to laxity (such as deregulation) which provokes a credit cycle, later to rigour (e.g., monetary tightening) that triggers a crisis;

2. Easing of entry conditions to financial markets, leading to heightened competition and risk taking;

3. Debt accumulation and asset price booms, generating vulnerable balance sheets in the financial and nonfinancial sectors;

4. Innovation in financial markets, which increases uncertainty during the crisis; and,

5. Risk concentration and lower capital adequacy for banks, which reduces robustness to shocks.

As Davis and Karim suggest, when all of these factors combine, financial instability and crisis are likely to ensue. In reviewing the evolution of subprime mortgaging, evidence of each of these factors appears to have been operating at some point before the system deteriorated. The pattern began with the subprime innovation, a largely untested and unpredictable financial product. The influx of unregulated brokerage firms, low/no documentation loans, relaxed underwriting standards (Foote et al., 2008), and record housing prices and equity accumulations represented a regime shift and an upward credit cycle. Entry conditions were eased for borrowers, brokers, lenders, securitizers and investors, which increased competition and risk taking. Housing values, processing volumes, and investment profits soared, while debt continued to accumulate across the board.[8] Finally, much of the risk became asymmetrical and concentrated within just a few segments of the mortgage finance industry. Nguyen and Pontell (2010:594) point out that a similar scenario unfolded in the savings and loan crisis in the 1980s.

Just as the risks associated with subprime lending were asymmetrical, so too were the direct and concentrated consequences of the crisis. Brokerages, banks, and investment firms have gone bankrupt, borrowers have lost their credit and homes due to default and foreclosure, and lenders, rating agencies, and the GSEs have been forced to reconsider and restructure their respective priorities and obligations. The indirect effects have been likewise considerable. Communities with excessive foreclosures are experiencing increased crime rates (Calem, Gillen & Wachter, 2004; Whitworth, 2008; Wilson & Paulson, 2008), global markets remain unpredictable and leery, the

---

[8] Aalbers (2009) explains that leveraging was a prime reason for the demise of the investment banks as they were funding their MBSs with borrowed money; small shifts in the performance of the securities would result in disproportionately larger profits and losses. With high leverage factors and the subprime meltdown, many of these firms quickly went bankrupt.

housing market is stagnant, credit is tight and interest rates remain low but unstable. Any one of these direct or indirect consequences of the subprime "boom and bust" could fill countless studies. Nevertheless, with a sufficient background now provided on the industry and its elementary operations, attention can now return to the primary objective of this section, which is to examine how fraud may have contributed to the destruction of the subprime industry in the United States.

Mortgage Fraud

Fraud comes in many forms and has been credited with playing a substantial role in the downfall of the subprime mortgage market over the past decade. Virtually all commentaries on the mortgage crisis have included some reference to the fraudulent activities of participants, ranging from the initial borrowers, all the way to the rating agencies, GSEs, and investors. Where each author places the blame is driven by their own perspectives on the empirical and anecdotal evidence, but all agree that many crossed the line from risky behavior to outright fraud in their pursuit of property or profit, and eventually the frauds became systemic (Patterson & Koller, 2011:33). The FBI (2011:5) defines mortgage fraud in the following manner:

> Mortgage fraud is a material misstatement, misrepresentation, or omission relied on by an underwriter or lender to fund, purchase, or insure a loan. This type of fraud is usually defined as loan origination fraud. Mortgage fraud also includes schemes targeting consumers, such as foreclosure rescue, short sale, and loan modification.

Table 2.3 provides a summary of the nature of fraud in the subprime industry as discussed in the emergent literature. As can be seen in this rudimentary typology, fraud in the mortgage industry has been perpetrated through material misrepresentations and manipulations across the board.

Table 2.3: Types of Fraud Reported in the Mortgage Process[9]

Participants	Fraudulent Activities
Borrowers	Misrepresentation of income, assets, liabilities & occupancy intentions; fabricated loans (straw buyers); identity theft
Brokers	Misrepresentation of borrower risk to lenders & of loan details to borrowers; manipulation of appraisals; massaging of or fabricated loans (straw buyers); identity theft
Appraisers	Overstating *or* understating property value
Homebuilders and Realtors	Appraisal manipulation; straw buyers; condominium conversions
Lenders	Misrepresentation of loan risk; massaging loans; deceptive accounting practices
Investment Banks	Misrepresentation of bundled loan risk; deceptive accounting practices
Government Sponsored Enterprises	Accounting manipulation; overvaluing capital position; overrating MBSs
Rating Agencies	Overrating non-agency MBSs; manipulative or defective statistical models

Adapted from Demyanyk (2009); FinCEN, 2006; and Landers et al. (2009).

The Financial Crimes Enforcement Network (FinCEN), an arm of the U.S. Department of the Treasury, also explains mortgage fraud in familiar white collar crime terms:

---

[9] Examples of fraud include application misrepresentations, deceptive appraisals and valuations, employment and deposit verifications, credit reports, tax returns/financial statements, and escrow/closing documents (MARI, 2011:9).

> Mortgage loan fraud can be divided into two broad categories: fraud for property and fraud for profit. Fraud for property generally involves material misrepresentation or omission of information with the intent to deceive or mislead a lender into extending credit that would likely not be offered if the true facts were known ... In contrast, the motivation behind fraud for profit is money. Fraud for profit is often committed with the complicity of industry insiders such as mortgage brokers, real estate agents, property appraisers, and settlement agents (attorneys and title examiners) (FinCEN, 2006:3).

FinCEN contends that these trends and patterns are supported by their analysis of thousands of Suspicious Activity Reports (SARs) filed over the years. SARs were originally designed to flag possible money laundering activity, but are now used by financial institutions to report any type of questionable transaction to FinCEN. SARs include subject (potential suspect), transaction, and institution details, and are intended to supply cursory information for the initiation of criminal investigations. When warranted, investigations can be arranged through a variety of law enforcement or regulatory bodies, such as the FBI, SEC, or IRS.

Like other capitalist business systems, the mortgage industry is built on motivation for property or profit, but predatory and fraudulent activity compromise the legitimate process (Landers et al., 2009).[10] Landers and colleagues explain that subprime lending becomes predatory when lenders target unqualified or undereducated potential borrowers (unethical) or fraudulent when misrepresentations occur (illegal). Yet home buyers are also motivated by the pursuit of property and profit, and thus predatory *borrowing* and consumer fraud is also commonplace.

---

[10] At higher levels, this could include "misstating and omitting key facts about a financial product," as alleged in the SEC charge against Goldman Sachs in 2010 (SEC, 2012).

In sum, individuals and organizations have been involved in a multitude of fraudulent practices through opportunities provided by the subprime mortgage process. How the motivations and opportunities for this fraud were generated is implicit in the economic literature; an application of criminological and diffusion perspectives in the next chapter will help to make this more explicit.

The Fallout

As with white collar crimes in general, the true extent of mortgage fraud is unknown and may never be fully understood. Several mechanisms, like SARs, are in place to improve the reporting and investigation of frauds, but the crimes must still be initially detected or uncovered. Although there is the possibility of reporting bias with mortgage fraud, the sheer volume and growth of the mortgage industry suggests that the number of fraud occurrences did rise significantly following the adoption of subprime lending strategies in the 1990s.

Figure 2.2: Estimated Value of Fraudulent Loans

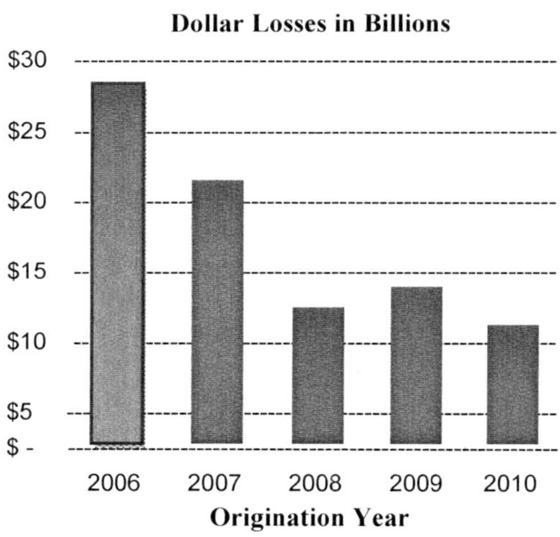

Source: FBI (2012:6; citing *Corelogic*).

FinCEN (2006) reported that depository institution SARs pertaining to mortgage loan fraud sharply increased in 2002 and continued to rise; SARs alleging mortgage fraud increased by 1411% between 1997 and 2005, comprising roughly 2% of total filings in 1997, and almost 5% in 2005. By the third quarter of 2011, mortgage loan fraud SARs accounted for 10% of all SARs filed since the final quarter of 2007 (FinCEN, 2012:2).

As stated previously, both the FBI and SEC report similar escalations in SARs and subsequent investigations. All told, the extent of fraud from a purely financial perspective is also staggering. Although estimates range depending on the source, Figure 2.2 gives a general idea of the scope of the problem: previous reports of mortgage fraud losses were recorded as totaling $429 million in 2004 and this rose to almost $1.5 billion by 2008 and $2.8 billion in 2009 (FBI, 2010). These figures continue to be updated and revised based on new data and are reflected in the updated table. The FBI (2012:6; citing *Corelogic*) now estimates that the dollar amount of estimated fraudulent loans (by origination year) exceeded $25 billion in 2006, with 2010 losses currently being estimated at over $10 billion.

CHAPTER 3

Toward an Understanding of Mortgage Fraud

Sutherland: Contributions and Connections

It appears that no discussion of white collar crime can begin or would be complete without the obligatory reference to Edwin Sutherland's contributions. This chapter will not stray from the tradition for a number of reasons. First, although genuine interest in white collar crime dates back to the turn of the 20th century, Sutherland is generally recognized as being responsible for bringing the issue of occupational and organizational crime to the surface of criminological discourse in the late 1930s (Braithwaite, 1985; Friedrichs, 2007; Geis, Meier, & Salinger, 1995; Shover & Hochstetler, 2006). It took a number of years following his initial introduction of the subject at the 1939 American Sociological Society annual meeting for Sutherland to more clearly articulate and refine his propositions. However, following the publication of his manuscript in 1949, the term *white collar crime* soon became common in the global vocabulary (Geis & Goff, 1983).

Geis and Goff (1983) credit Sutherland for helping to broach and refine the definition of white collar crime, spurring decades of scholarly work on the subject and raising the sophistication level of debate on the causes of crime and criminality. Granted, definitional (e.g., offender vs. offense-based definitions – see Edelhertz, 1970) and empirical challenges continue to this day, and although the topic has its share of critics, and has had its share of fits and starts, most contemporary scholars would agree that white collar crime retains a unique position in criminological thought, dialogue, and inquiry.

Second, Sutherland was writing on the heels of one of the greatest "boom" and "bust" periods of the 20th century. The corollaries between the economic events of the 1920s (e.g., speculative spending, risk-taking, housing crisis, role of brokers and regulation) and those of the 1990s/2000s discussed above are striking. One has to wonder if Sutherland's white collar crime concerns *had* been more immediately and fully articulated and investigated, rather than minimized for years due to a conservative political climate (Geis & Goff, 1983), would history had to have repeated itself? It is possible that a more thorough understanding of the current mortgage crisis, how it developed, and what could have been done to prevent it, may reduce further repetitions.

Third, although Sutherland may not have completely made the theoretical connections between each of the social, psychological, political, and structural conditions that contribute to crime (Friedrichs, 2007), he did stimulate concern for how these factors interact. Rather than adopting a purely Classical or Positivist perspective[11] on crime or criminality, Sutherland also advanced the field by highlighting the notion of direct and vicarious learning processes. With his argument that criminal behavior is learned just like any other behavior, his view steered away from purely biological or pathological explanations, and was consistent with the developing social and cognitive learning approaches being refined during the mid-1900s.

Furthermore, Sutherland advanced the work of Shaw and McKay (1942) in his efforts to separate the structural or contextual conditions (what he referred to as "differential social organization") from the

---

[11] The Classical or "free will" perspective is built on the assumption that man is a rational being and engages in crime to maximize pleasure and minimize pain. The Positivist perspective suggests that social conditions external to the individual (e.g., environment, family, peers) contribute to the likelihood that an individual will engage in crime.

processes that impact whether or not an individual learns and ultimately participates in criminal activities. These "differential association" processes provided the foundations of his perspective by identifying the "mechanisms that explain the genesis of crime regardless of the specific structural, social, and individual conditions involved" (Matsueda, 1988:277). The insightful and integrative nature of Sutherland's framework should not be minimized.

Fourth and finally, as stated in Chapter 1, Sutherland (1983:246) claims that the *diffusion* of illegal practices is "evidence that white collar crime is due to differential association" and is generally the result of the pursuit of profit maximization by individuals involved in business activities. In addition to how knowledge and techniques of how to take advantage of opportunities spread, general attitudes and cognitions similarly diffuse, and in combination this overall transmission helps to explain the presence and resulting weight of definitions favorable to law violations. Moving past mere semantics, the "diffusion" idea evident in Sutherland's theory has arguably not been fully developed from an opportunity perspective.[12] For example, it is shown below that the structure and availability of opportunities is critical to the facilitation of white collar crime, but understanding how these opportunities actually develop and spread, particularly in the mortgage industry, cannot be explained by conventional criminological theories alone.

In sum, Sutherland's contributions are relevant to the current investigation on a number of fronts. Besides his introduction of white collar crime into criminological discourse, he boldly confronted sensitive economic and political issues during the aftermath of a devastating financial catastrophe which in large part was reportedly fueled by greed and fraud. Furthermore, Sutherland adopted an integrative theoretical framework from which to approach the study of

---

[12] Shapiro (1990) noted a similar oversight with Sutherland's concept of violations of "trust" in that prior to her investigation scholars had not pursued this "promising" lead.

crime and criminality, and introduced the notion that diffusion plays a critical role in the transmission of criminal motivation and opportunity. In light of the current global fiscal crisis and state of economic affairs, this is precisely the right time for criminologists to more fully capitalize on and advance these contributions.

Similar to other social and behavioral phenomena, approaching the study of white collar crime is no easy task, on either theoretical or empirical grounds (Friedrichs, 2007; Shover & Wright, 2001). For instance, Cullen and Agnew (2002) outline at least sixteen different theoretical perspectives, each of which is accompanied by a uniquely applicable empirical framework. Without adopting a sophisticated integrated approach (e.g., see Coleman, 1987) to study subprime mortgage fraud, deciding which theoretical perspective(s) to adopt is arguably only constrained by the imagination and personal preferences of the scholar. As will be outlined below, however, it is precisely this type of integrated approach (which includes a non-traditional perspective) which may be necessary to account for the multitude of factors associated with white collar crime in the form of subprime mortgage fraud.

Opportunity

It is well understood that motivation and opportunity play important roles in crime. As Coleman (1987:406) suggests, criminal behavior "results from the confluence of appropriate motivation and opportunity," and to understand white collar crime both aspects of behavior must be accounted for. Coleman (p. 409) adheres to the following definitions in this regard:

> Motivation consist(s) of a set of symbolic constructions defining certain kinds of goals and activities as appropriate and desirable and others as lacking those qualities. An opportunity is defined as a potential course of action, made possible by a particular set of social conditions, which has been symbolically incorporated into an actor's *repertoire* of behavior possibilities. Thus, a potential course of action becomes an opportunity only when someone is aware of it.

The motivation for fraud is associated with an illegal quest for profit or property (FinCEN, 2006) or other personal or organizational gain (National White Collar Crime Center, 2008). Motivation is arguably a critical element of most crimes. In fact, *mens rea*, or guilty intent, is a statutory element requiring proof in many criminal offense prosecutions (see Cressey, 1989, for a counterargument). What distinguishes white collar crime (particularly for fraud) from conventional crime motivation and intentions, however, is arguably the basic or simple pursuit of either material or monetary gain. As such, motivation, or the "why" factor, is almost a given in explanations of white collar *criminality*, yet it still must be accounted for in any criminological discussion designed to move beyond the basic opportunity structure of the *criminal event*.

Along with motivation, opportunity, or the "how" factor, must also be addressed to understand the ways in which criminal intentions are carried out through criminal events. For as Grabosky and Shover (2010:649) point out, opportunities "are only as good as those who would exploit them." Benson and Simpson (2009) explain the opportunity structure of white collar crime and that there are three techniques and three properties which distinguish white collar crime from other types of conventional crime (e.g., street or violent crime). They also contend that the trickery involved in fraudulent activity is manifested in the general and intentional techniques used in the commission of white collar crime (the means/methods for accomplishing some desired aim). These activities are distinct from many techniques found in conventional crime (e.g., the use of weapons or force). These white collar crime strategies include deception, abuse of trust, and concealment or conspiracy.

"Deception occurs when one person misleads another by making things appear other than as they really are" (Benson & Simpson, 2009:81); fraudulent material misrepresentations are a classic case of deception. To accomplish deception, which is motivated by profit, property, or other gain, white collar criminals in some way abuse the trust instilled in them by virtue of their role in exchange relationships or by some other violation of their fiduciary responsibilities (National

White Collar Crime Center, 2008). Moreover, Benson and Simpson explain that concealment and conspiracy are used to hide the crimes so no one even knows they have been committed. By imitating legitimate business activities, criminal events are hidden in such a way that the crime and its effects may not even be detected. These techniques once again distinguish white collar crime from conventional crime; in the latter, concealment and conspiracy are motivated by attempts to hide the identity of the offender, not necessarily the crime itself.

Besides techniques, white collar crime also includes specific properties (Benson & Simpson, 2009) which help to define an individual's potential courses of action. These include specialized access (offender has legitimate access to the target and location in which the crime is committed), the superficial appearance of legitimacy (victims and guardians may never know that a crime has been committed; offenders use their occupational positions to take advantage of legitimate activities in illegal ways) and spatial separation from victims (offenses generally do not include any direct contact with the victim; facilitates the invisibility of the crime). Benson and Simpson argue that of these properties, specialized access is the key to white collar offenses – it is precisely the offender's position in a particular occupational or organizational role that provides access to crime opportunities and targets. It further helps offenders mask their illegal activities as legitimate and allows them to maintain spatial separation from their victims.

Just as specialized access sets up the other properties, it also gives the offender the chance to use the techniques required for successful involvement in white collar crime (Benson and Simpson, 2009). In contrast, conventional crime activities do not have this type of routine access. For example, an offender may have to commit an initial crime just to gain access to a target, such as "breaking and entering" to commit a theft (burglary), or may need to use force or the threat of force to reach and secure the ultimate target of their intentions (e.g., robbery for property). As such, rarely would the activities surrounding a conventional crime be construed as legitimate.

Spatial separation is also rare with conventional crime. As many potential victims use active and passive strategies (e.g., traveling in groups, alarms, anti-theft devices) to protect themselves and their property from conventional crime, direct contact is more likely as offenders must overcome these physical barriers to reach their targets. This also explains why the techniques and properties of white collar crime have varying degrees of importance depending on the type of offense being committed. Similar to conventional crime (e.g., rape or auto theft), each type of white collar crime (e.g., fraud, embezzlement, price-fixing, or bribery) has a unique opportunity structure and accompanying properties, requiring offenders to utilize different combinations of techniques to accomplish their goals. Although the offenses arguably have the same property categories and utilize the same techniques, specific forms of white collar crime need to be investigated individually to uncover the relative weight of these aspects (Benson et al., 2009).

Associations

As stated previously, the criminological theory of "differential association" was first articulated by Sutherland during the mid-1900s. The thesis set forth by Sutherland (1983) centers implicitly on direct and vicarious learning processes, and the belief that criminal behavior is learned just like any other behavior. He argued:

> The hypothesis of differential association is that criminal behavior is learned in association with those who define such criminal behavior favorably and in isolation from those who define it unfavorably, and that a person in an appropriate situation engages in such criminal behavior if, and only if, the weight of the favorable definitions exceeds the weight of the unfavorable definitions (Sutherland, 1983:240).

Sutherland explained that an individual's associations vary in frequency, duration, priority, and intensity, and help to explain not only juvenile delinquency and street crime, but white collar crime as well. These types of illegal behavior involve the same process of exposure to, and interaction with, significant others who may or may not favor law-abiding views and behavior. For example, similar to street crime hot spots, the evidence reveals that mortgage fraud tends to be clustered geographically, suggesting that the likelihood of individual mortgage practitioners being involved in fraud may be correlated with the extent and nature of their local business interactions and environment, in which they may come into contact with others involved in mortgage scams (Calem, Gillen, & Wachter, 2004).

With respect to motivation and opportunity, Sutherland conceptualized motivation as stemming from the adoption of an excess of definitions (e.g., attitudes, values, techniques, rationalizations, beliefs) from associations which are favorable to law-violating. In this sense, the definitions facilitate motivation by encouraging and freeing the individual to engage in criminal behavior.[13] For example, Sykes and Matza (1957) extend Sutherland's concept of "rationalizations" which contribute to an offender's justification for involvement in illegal behavior. They contend the *content* of what is learned is as important as the process by which it is learned (through association with a delinquent subculture), arguing that despite involvement in illegal activity, many delinquents feel guilt and shame about their behavior and may otherwise highly regard prosocial values. Therefore, to free themselves to violate the legal and social norms they may actually believe in, delinquents must justify participating in the behavior to

---

[13] Clarke and Cornish (1985:147) argue properly specified models of criminal behavior must be specific to particular types of crime and must then separately "describe both the processes of involvement in crime and the decisions surrounding the commission of the offense itself." Clarke and Cornish also tend to generally minimize the importance of deviance, biological and/or psychological explanations for crime, placing their perspective rather within the realm of the Classical school of thought (e.g., man as a rational being). Their rational choice theory is deterrence-based and driven by the concepts of bounded rationality and expected utility, as well as other dynamic cognitive processes such as techniques of neutralization. It also makes "no hard-and-fast distinction between offenders and the law-abiding" (Clarke & Cornish, 2001:33). Rather simply, individuals choose to participate in crime if the benefits outweigh the costs.

relieve this guilt or shame. Sykes and Matza explain this practice of rationalizing can follow *or* precede the behavior, and although they do not explain criminal motivation, these scholars help to reveal that distinct cognitions or beliefs are needed to support and carry out criminal objectives.[14]

These types of cognitive tactics have been substantiated for a variety of criminal offenders, including violent offenders (Agnew, 1994). They have also been applied to white collar criminals, with a finding that a "denial of criminal intent" helps offenders compensate for past involvement in illegal activities (Benson, 1985). In contrast, Hamlin (1988) contends that techniques of neutralization are actually post-facto "motives" used to legitimate prior involvement in crime, claiming that motives are produced only after the acts have been committed and need to be defended. Benson (1985) also found that the denial of intent was more of an after-the-fact response for explaining

---

[14] Cognitions are also a component of rational choice theory (Clarke & Cornish, 1985). However, Nagin and Paternoster (1993) criticize the lack of attention to individual differences as a missing component of rational choice theory, providing evidence that although individuals may have similar motives, they differ in their propensity to offend and how they interpret choices (risk/benefit conclusions). Bouffard (2007) also explains that there is a difference between perceptual and objective assessments of risk and benefits (similar to what is argued in contemporary deterrence theory) and these have ramifications for crime policy. An individual's assessment of risk and opportunities is dynamic (e.g., changing ability to process information; tolerance for personal or formal sanctions) which suggests deeper cognitive processes may be at work than what can be reasonably explained by the assumptions of rational choice theory (Piliavin, Gartner, Thornton, & Matsueda, 1986). Individuals also possess different levels of self-control, have varying social bonds, and may encounter crime opportunities at different time frames in their lives. In sum, failing to account for these individual differences weakens the viability of rational choice theory – theoretically, empirically, and practically.

criminal involvement, but these rationalizations are arguably not the same as original motivations.

Benson and Simpson (2009) point out that differential interactions and exposures can stimulate white collar criminal motivation and intent in a number of ways. For example, the culture of business can be criminogenic as it may not promote ethics, morality or obedience to the law (crime may be a way of doing business); and, attitudes and rationalizations may be cultivated through the socialization process in which favorable definitions of law violation outweigh unfavorable definitions.[15] Zyglidopoulus, Fleming, and Rothenberg (2009) concur, arguing that individuals engaged in corruption use learned rationalizations as defense mechanisms to alleviate guilt and to justify their past and potential involvement in unethical or illegal behavior. They illustrate the bigger problem is that when these behaviors are consistently overcompensated for, or over-rationalized, the ideology of the corporate environment may become criminogenic, and corruption escalates (see also Ashforth & Anand, 2003; Patterson & Koller, 2011).

In sum, although these renditions of differential association begin to compensate for what "definitions" consist of and how they spread through associations, they do not address the underlying motivation for increased property or profit (e.g., what relative advantages does property or profit give?; can crime provide this advantage?), or what mechanisms are needed for the actual transmission of the definitions. It will be demonstrated in the following chapter that the diffusion of innovations perspective may be well suited to fill these gaps. Furthermore, opportunity is more of an assumed criterion in Sutherland's definition, as the individual must simply be "in an appropriate situation" for a criminal event to occur. Granted, Sutherland does further articulate that individuals learn "definitions of

---

[15] Manhattan District Attorney Vance alleged precisely this type of criminogenic culture in a press release following the sentencing of AFG Financial Group principals in a $100 million mortgage fraud case: "Crime was the business of AFG – these four defendants went to work every day with the intent to commit mortgage fraud; it was literally their job" (NY.gov, 2010).

situations in which those techniques may be used" (1983:245) and does explore how diffusion of illegal practices spread through associations. Most of his discussions are devoted to anecdotal accounts, however, and as stated previously, he never fully clarifies how this diffusion process originates or operates.

Benson and Simpson (2009) aptly point out that techniques (e.g., how to spot and take advantage of opportunities) are learned in the socialization process, and there may be a lack of institutional organization against misconduct (e.g., when opportunities can be freely taken advantage of with minimal risk of detection). Once again, however, this interpretation of differential association appears wanting in that it does not account for the spread of opportunities across organizations[16] within an industry or system in which socialization or exposure to definitions may be less formal or direct.[17]

In conclusion, Sutherland's differential association theory provides a useful starting point for the examination of subprime mortgage fraud,

---

[16] One of Cressey's (1989) main points is that it is impossible to measure both individual and corporate actions under one causal behavioral theory; making the distinction between occupational and corporate crime (Clinard & Quinney, 1973; Clinard & Yeager, 1978) does not make this exercise any more palatable (i.e., organizations do not "behave"). Yet one could similarly argue that the distinction is precisely what identifies the party maintaining the white collar crime *motivation*; either motivation for individual gain, or the motivation for organizational benefit. It will be demonstrated that diffusion of innovations theory also suggests different models for individual and organizational innovation-decision processes.

[17] Coleman (1987) does expand on this issue. He notes three distinct subcultures exist within an occupational setting with each providing attitudes, beliefs, definitions, and normative standards: organizational (the corporation), industry (the business/social system), and the occupational (the career). Coleman argues the combination of these subcultures and the associations they encourage isolate its members from mainstream life and ideology.

and its emphasis on personal interactions is consistent with the diffusion of innovations perspective (see Chapter 4). Clinard and coauthors (1973, 1978), Cressey (1989), and Sykes and Matza (1957) have helped to clarify the theory, but others maintain that it still falls short in accounting for all of the motives, opportunities, and processes involved in criminal behavior.[18]

In Sutherland's defense, if he had made a clearer distinction between his theories on white collar crime and differential association, or they were more separated in space and time, many of these arguments may have been mute. Regardless, and despite Cressey's (1989) condemnations, further advancements continue to be made, such as through the work of Benson (1985), Agnew (1994), and Zyglidopoulus, Fleming, and Rothenberg (2009). These theoretical advancements, for example, provide explanations of how a business culture can become criminogenic. As such, they may complement the examination of how fraud in the subprime market diffused and became so endemic in the United States.

Routines

In contrast to Differential Association and other Social Learning theories, the "Routine Activities" perspective *assumes* motivation (and a ready supply of offenders) and does not attempt to explain it (Felson, 2001). The primary impetus for Routine Activity Theory is to explain

---

[18] The *process* component of Sutherland's theory has also been extended with the "differential association-reinforcement" theory of criminal behavior (Burgess & Akers, 1966). This theory later evolved into what is now referred to as "social learning" theory (Akers, 1990; Akers, 1996). The differential association-reinforcement perspective reformulated differential association theory to integrate it with the behavioral principles of learning in an attempt to explain what the actual mechanisms of learning are. Burgess and Akers believed that the original precepts of differential association failed to account for the reinforcement and contingency properties of operant conditioning, which they argue are essential in the transmission, evocation and maintenance of behavior – unconventional or otherwise.

how a variety of factors must coalesce for a criminal event to occur, and as such it can be construed as an environmental or situational theory about crime rather than one about criminality per se (Clarke, 1980). The causal organization of the theory by Cohen and Felson (1979) was originally applied to direct-contact predatory crimes (personal or property) and suggests that the probability of a criminal event is based on the convergence in time and space of a motivated offender and a suitable target, in a place in which there is an absence of a capable guardian to protect the target.

The basic concept of the theory holds simply that offenders differentially encounter situations and potential opportunities for crime (i.e., suitable targets in places with an absence of capable guardians) based on the activities of their and their potential victims' daily routines. These situations are also structured differentially with respect to environmental conditions, such as population density and mobility, weather conditions, time of day, setting (e.g., residential or commercial) and the like. For example, Cohen and Felson (1979) explain that the very factors which contribute to increased daily personal activities (e.g., automobiles, women in the workforce, durable products) also facilitate increased opportunities for crime and victimization. As such, routine activities theory is a useful perspective with which to approach the study of aggregate victimization and crime rates (e.g., auto theft, female crime, theft) over time and place (e.g., urban, suburban, rural). It may also help to explain why subprime mortgage fraud is concentrated geographically (Calem et al., 2004; Carswell & Bachtel, 2007) or within certain segments of the industry.

Benson et al. (2009) specifically apply routine activities and its complementary crime pattern theory to the white collar crime opportunity perspective (see above). These authors note that the three conditions required for white collar crime differ somewhat from those found in conventional crime, and that the necessary elements of white collar crime include "the offenders, the victims, and the existing occupational or organizational feature(s) that facilitate contact between the victim and offender" (p. 179). Therefore, the notion of "place" is reconceptualized as including the networks and processes that are involved in exchange relationships as well as other situations in which offenders can use techniques to capitalize on the properties of white collar crime (i.e., specialized access, the superficial appearance of legitimacy, and spatial separation from victims).

Thus, even though routine activities theory was originally applied to direct-contact predatory crimes, it has also shown increased utility for examining and explaining indirect-contact crimes. Its consistency with the opportunity perspective provides a rich framework for examining how individuals and aggregates might take advantage of occupational, organizational, and industrial routines and their potentially rewarding crime opportunities, and in turn how these very opportunities may ultimately be restructured to diminish the likelihood of crime.

As implied throughout this chapter, crime and criminal behavior have been interpreted as resulting from individual choice and proclivities, to structural and contextual factors. The criminological challenge to date seems to have been to identify the theory, or combination of theories, which have the most utility in explaining the phenomenon of white collar crime. This challenge has been hampered, however, as: (1) most traditional criminological theories were developed with the basic delinquent or street criminal in mind; (2) the population of white collar criminals does not lend itself well to study (see Benson & Simpson, 2009); and, (3) no conceptual and/or empirical model which can compensate for all of the factors (e.g., motivation, opportunity, personal proclivities, associations, routines) associated with white collar crime has been fully articulated to date.

In contrast to conventional crime then, the illegal behavior of individuals and organizations involved in otherwise legitimate business activities does not fit nicely into one particular theory or "school of thought." It has been implied that traditional criminological theory is limited to the extent that it can explain white collar crime and criminality, much less the specific crime of subprime mortgage fraud. This suggests the new challenge then is to integrate the primary components of the theories (e.g., opportunity, associations and routines) and to investigate and apply a non-criminological perspective to help compensate for these theoretical, conceptual, practical, and empirical limitations. It is to this latter challenge that the discussion will now turn.

CHAPTER 4

Diffusion of Innovation

> Simply put: innovation isn't what innovators *do*; it's what customers, clients, and people *adopt*. Innovation isn't about crafting brilliant ideas that change minds; it's about the distribution of usable artifacts that change behavior. Innovators – their optimistic arrogance withstanding – don't change the world; the users of their innovations do. That's not a subtle distinction (Schrage, 2004).

Although the source of innovations (Schrage's "innovators"), and the ideas, motivations, and intentions of their creators are of interest and ultimate relevance, these issues are not readily apparent with respect to the subprime mortgage industry.[19] For example, Apgar and Herbert

---

[19] This origination or "generation of innovations" is complex and multidimensional, although the distinction between a product and a process innovation (Berente, Yoo & Lyytinen, 2008) is somewhat blurred with respect to the subprime mortgage. As such, the mortgage tool, and the practices and routines it effects, will continue to be interpreted simply as the present innovation of interest, and the discussion will instead focus primarily on the users of these innovations (legitimately and illegitimately), as well as on the factors that influenced how, why, and how quickly they chose to adopt them.

(2006:*vii*) note that a thorough literature review suggests "surprisingly little is known about the factors that have given rise in recent years to products and services as diverse as subprime mortgage loans." To be sure, some of these factors and the history of subprime lending were outlined in Chapter 2, yet how the innovative product/service itself spread throughout the mortgage industry, and why it has been accompanied by unprecedented levels of fraud, remains to be revealed. For reasons to be illuminated below, the diffusion of innovations tradition may provide the ideal framework with which to assess and interpret these phenomena further.

Origins of Diffusion Theory

Diffusion research is first noted to have been undertaken in Europe in the early 1900s, was subjected to further development by Ryan and Gross in the U.S. in the 1940s, and was eventually synthesized by Everett Rogers in 1962 (Kincaid, 2004). The viability of Rogers' articulated diffusion research paradigm continues to this day. As Hornik (2004) suggests, Rogers' original work has provided a stable core view of diffusion of innovations, yet over time Rogers' models have been responsive to changing perspectives as other scholarly communities have applied it to a wide range of innovations.

As stated previously, a variety of disciplines have successfully utilized diffusion theory over the past fifty years, including the fields of anthropology, sociology, social psychology, education, communication, marketing and management, public relations, and geography (Rogers, 2003). For example, the theory has guided the study of everything from how physicians learn about and adopt new prescription medicine regimes (Coleman, Katz, & Menzel, 1957), to what factors influence the adoption of new strategies and policies by police departments (Weiss, 1997). In fact, Kincaid (2004) claims diffusion of innovations is not really a theory; rather, it is a model or general framework making it amenable to this variety of cross-discipline applications. He contends the comprehensiveness and generalizability of the model are at once its strength and weakness, yet its adaptability has enabled the perspective to remain sensitive to contemporary use and discourse, and has encouraged its continued applicability in the social and behavioral sciences.

Rogers (2003) notes the appeal of the diffusion research paradigm for understanding human behavior change is predicated on four factors: (1) its conceptual framework has multidisciplinary relevance; (2) it provides an applied scheme of analyzing social problems and potential solutions; (3) it empirically allows for higher-level theoretical generalizations; and, (4) its suggested methodology (e.g., data collection and analysis) is clear cut and relatively easy to use. Although Rogers admits these very factors can also inhibit theoretical advancements, many argue this should not limit or inhibit its use in the study of innovation diffusion phenomena.

The Diffusion Process

Prior to a brief review of the diffusion process, a few definitions and clarifications are warranted. *Diffusion* is defined by Rogers (2003:5) as the "process in which an innovation is communicated through certain channels over time among the members of a social system." As such, the diffusion of innovations involves the interaction of four primary factors: an innovation, communication channels, a social system, and time (Rogers; Haider & Kreps, 2004).

Diffusion includes both the planned and spontaneous spread of new ideas; the *social system* which adopts the new idea is the set of interrelated units engaged in joint problem solving to accomplish common goals (Rogers, 2003). Rogers further defines *communication* as a "process in which participants create and share information with one another in order to reach a mutual understanding" (p. 5) and an *innovation* as an "idea, practice, or object that is perceived as new by an individual or other unit of adoption" (p. 12). In sum, diffusion of innovations theory[20] is concerned with the social change that occurs as

---

[20] Hornik (2004) describes "diffusion of innovations" as a framework, and implies "diffusion" is the theory. Kincaid (2004) is also reluctant to consider

new information is transferred among and between similar decision-making units, and how various mechanisms and conditions influence the transmission and adoption process.

Innovation-Decision

The transmission of ideas and the stages of reflection and change which accompany it (Hornik, 2004) are diagrammed in Figure 4.1, with the *innovation-diffusion* process being defined as:

> The process through which an individual (or other decision-making unit) passes from first knowledge of an innovation, to forming an attitude toward the innovation, to a decision to adopt or reject, to implementation of the new idea, and to confirmation of this decision (Rogers, 2003:170).

As illustrated in Figure 4.1, a decision-making unit, assisted by the transfer of information through communication channels, progresses through the innovation-decision process stages (i.e., knowledge, persuasion, decision, implementation, and confirmation) over time in a predictable manner. Hornik (2004) contends that the traditional diffusion focus has been on the external influences operating at these various stages, yet there are differential internal influences (psychological) operating as well; in combination, these forces and information sources help to explain the ultimate adoption, rejection,

---

diffusion of innovations a theory, and even Rogers (2004) describes it as a model. Nevertheless, the term "theory" has been and will continue to be applied interchangeably with "model" to the diffusion of innovations concept throughout this study to facilitate a common frame of reference. The term "paradigm" is used herein to describe the overall framework/school of thought on diffusion and is consistent with Rogers' terminology.

Figure 4.1: Five-Stage Innovation-Decision Process

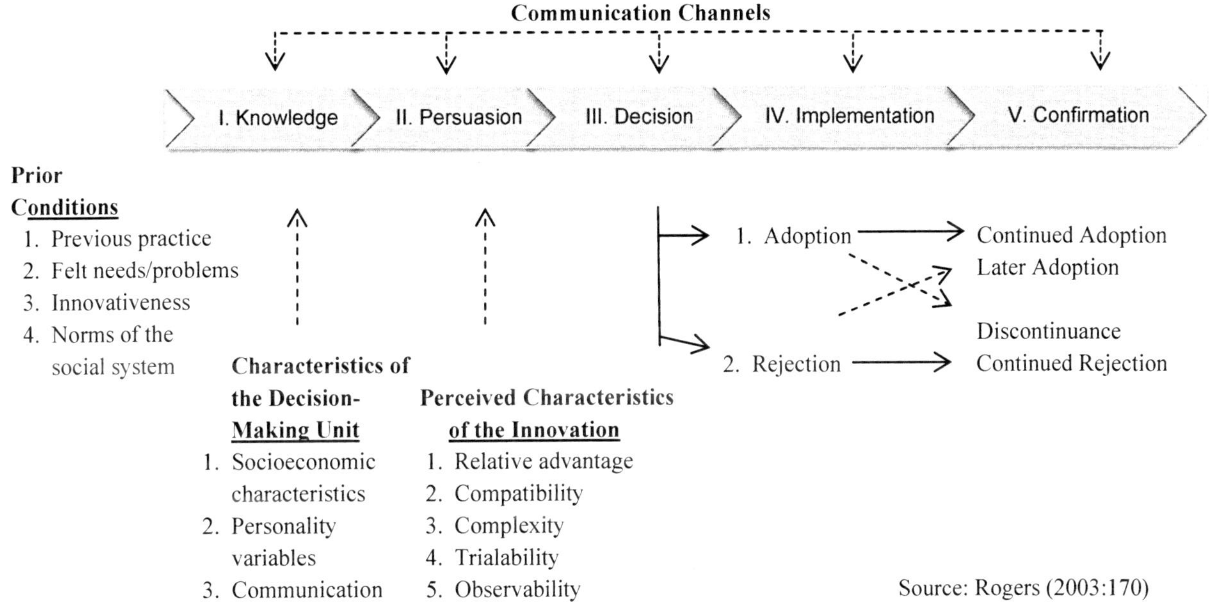

Source: Rogers (2003:170)

later adoption, or discontinued use of an innovation.[21]

Figure 4.1 represents the theoretical model of how individuals go from first knowledge of a new idea to confirming their own decision to use or reject the innovation.[22] The process can be examined by what takes place during each stage, such as what activities the individuals are involved in, what they must consider, the choices they need to make, what influences their cognitions, emotions, and behaviors, and what needs to happen before they continue on to the next stage. Rogers (2003) asserts the activities associated with the process are influenced by prior conditions (e.g., previous practice, felt needs/problems, innovativeness, and social system norms) and communication channels. The stages also reflect the nature of individuals to evaluate important things *rationally*, and to partake in uncertainty avoidance when confronted with new ideas. Therefore, each stage in the cumulative

---

[21] Hornik (2004) argues the innovation-decision process model should not be approached too simplistically. For example, he stresses that contrary to some claims that formal communication channels only influence awareness, and informal channels only become influential at the later stages, behavior change can be influenced by any or no source depending on the combination of all the other relevant explanatory factors. Yet again, the model is relatively straightforward and broadly applicable.

[22] Rogers (2003) and Hornik (2004) assess the similarities between the innovation-decision process and the newer communication discipline's "stages-of-change" model of Prochaska, DiClemente, and Norcross (1992: In search of how people change: Applications to addictive behaviors. *American Psychologist*, *47*:1102-1114). They report this latter model also has five stages, consisting of precontemplation, contemplation, preparation, action, and maintenance. Although the stages-of-change model attends to the cognitive processes associated with behavioral change and may be useful at a later time, the work was not reviewed here as it does not address the actual diffusion of ideas, and Rogers suggests its applicability is still being investigated. Note these stages are also similar to those identified in rational choice theory by Clarke and Cornish (1985).

decision-making process also represents a potential rejection point of the entire idea, with the time it takes from "awareness-knowledge" to "decision" reflecting the actual innovation-decision period (time to adoption/rejection).

Rate of Adoption

Rogers (2003) explains the length of the innovation-decision process varies by innovation, and the awareness-knowledge rate is more rapid than the adoption rate of an innovation, as the rate of adoption, or the speed at which members of a social system adopt the innovation, is dependent on a larger variety of factors (see Figure 4.2). These factors include the perceived attributes of the innovation, the type of innovation-decision, communication channels, the nature of the social system, and the extent of change agents' promotion efforts. Of these, the perceived attributes of an innovation (e.g., relative advantage, compatibility, complexity, trialability, and observability) generally account for more rate of adoption variance, across all types of innovations, than all other factors combined (Rogers, 2003).

Although the strength of innovation attributes does not minimize the importance of the other structural or contextual variables, it does demonstrate that it is the perceived and subjective characteristics of the actual idea, practice, or object which influence decision-makers and how quickly it is adopted. Rogers (2003) notes, however, the specific characteristics of innovations influencing rate of adoption may include many more than these five general attributes; he warns that it behooves the researcher to identify these other factors rather than making implicit assumptions that they are exclusive, exhaustive or even universally generalizable. For example, Mansfield (1961) found that profitability was a major influence on the rate of adoption for many organizational innovations, and this factor has been repeatedly demonstrated (Diamond, 2003).

For a variety of reasons, the type of innovation-decision (e.g., optional, collective, or authority) also influences how quickly an innovation is adopted within social systems. For example, an individual

Figure 4.2: Variables Determining the Rate of Adoption

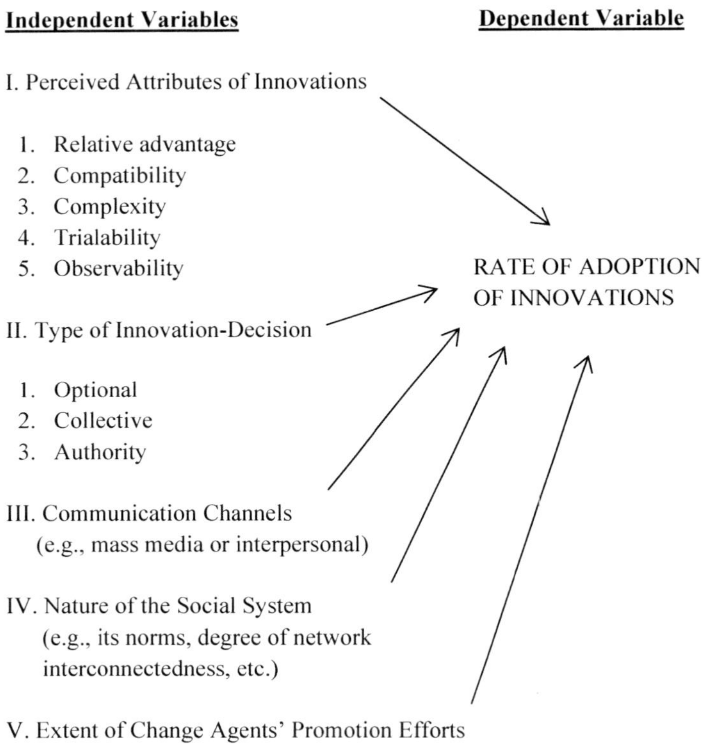

Source: Adapted from Rogers (2003:222)

-optional innovation-decision process proceeds and adoption occurs more rapidly than when organizational individuals resist mandates to comply with a new way of doing things, or when more individuals are involved, as is the case with more involved collective innovation-decisions. Peer or authority pressure also influences adoption rates, as do the nature, norms, and culture of the system and its networks (Strang & Soule, 1998). Measuring the rate of adoption is dependent on the availability of information, and the form of the distribution depends on the speed of the diffusion as well as the degree to which the adoption process has progressed at the time it is being measured (Valente, 2005).

Figure 4.3 illustrates the general cumulative S-shaped curve (based on time) of the typical innovation diffusion, and extends from the time of the innovation introduction (first knowledge), through the times at which certain cumulative percentages of the social system have adopted the innovation, to the time the diffusion process is complete and self-sustaining. The S-shaped rate of adoption curve is consistently found across innovations (Mahajan & Peterson, 1985; Rogers, 2003), although Valente (2005) found evidence that more centralized social networks tend to reach critical mass (point when the diffusion escalates) and sustainability quicker than decentralized or random networks.

For example, Westphal, Gulati, and Shortell (1997) found that the rate of adoption of "total quality management" programs by U.S. hospitals in the 1980s-1990s had a slow start and it was not until a national demonstration took place that critical mass was reached and the diffusion took off in earnest. Based on preliminary evidence, the subprime mortgage may have similarly reached critical mass due to the aftermath of 9/11; this will be further addressed in later chapters.

Figure 4.3: Adoption Curve and Adopter Categories

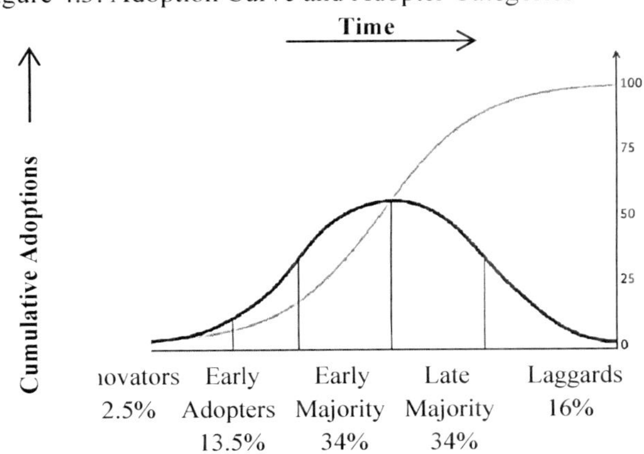

Adapted from: Mahajan & Peterson (1985) and Rogers (2003)

In sum, although an S-shaped (or other form) distribution time to adoption curve can be hypothesized depending on pre-study information and data, the researcher must let the data speak themselves.[23] The cumulative adoption curve, based on adopter distributions, may be more normal or bell-shaped (Rogers, 2003). Yet due to the consistent reliability of the curve, if there is an unusual spike in the distribution, such as that found by Westphal et al. (1997), this may reflect an influential event that should be investigated further. These types of spikes will also most likely be evident in the subprime distribution, not only due to the speed at which critical mass was reached in the early 2000s but also the result of the speed at which the critical mass *exodus* occurred in 2007.

Innovations

Regardless of decision-making processes or levels of potential adopter innovativeness, the characteristics of the actual innovations have much more influence on whether and when individuals and organizations adopt (Rogers, 2003). As illustrated previously, these innovation attributes contribute to adopter motivation (persuasion) and to the rate at which cumulative adoption occurs. The attributes are defined by Rogers as follows:

1. *Relative Advantage*: the degree to which an innovation is perceived as being better than the idea that supersedes it; often expressed as economic profitability or even social prestige.

2. *Compatibility*: the degree to which an innovation is perceived as consistent with the existing values, past experiences, and needs of potential adopters; more compatible equals less uncertainty.

---

[23] The cumulative rate of organizational innovation adoption is based on the same types of "innovation" characteristics and also generally results in an S-shaped curve distribution, suggesting that diffusion occurs in a similar pattern regardless of the level of the unit of analysis (e.g., individual, aggregate) (Rogers, 2003).

3. *Complexity*: the degree to which an innovation is perceived as relatively difficult to understand and use; may be a barrier to adoption if too complex.

4. *Trialability*: the degree to which an innovation may be experimented with on a limited basis; may involve breaking the innovation down or reinvention.

5. *Observability*: the degree to which the results of an innovation are visible to others; this relates to direct and vicarious reinforcement.

As described, the perceptual utility of an innovation is also more important than its actual utility. Haider and Kreps (2004:4) suggest the "optimization of these five qualities will allow an innovation to be adopted more rapidly than other innovations that lack them." As such, innovation originators have some control over how likely and quickly their products or practices are likely to be adopted – for example, through "ease of use" designs or the formal communication of demonstrable benefits. Attention to these attributes, and how the innovation-decision processes operate on the individual and organizational levels, should also inform innovators and communicators (change agents) as to the potential desirable and undesirable, direct/indirect, and anticipated/unanticipated consequences of diffused innovations (Haider & Kreps). These originators should also consider and be aware of how attention or inattention to these characteristics might influence the likelihood of reinvention by adopters.

Reinvention

Reinvention is defined as "the degree to which an innovation is changed or modified by a user in the process of its adoption and implementation" (Rogers, 2003:180). Rogers explains the concept of reinvention was not seriously recognized by diffusion researchers until the 1970s. Until that time, it was assumed that innovations were purely and passively imitated; any deviations of their use were attributable to unusual behavior, and these cases would be treated as mere outliers. However, as researchers discovered and admitted reinvention occurred and that it occurred regularly (it was not an anomaly), they began to investigate it more fully. Indeed, the generalizability of an innovation has been found to lead to faster rates of adoption and higher degrees of sustainability, so reinvention may be intentionally (or unintentionally) encouraged by design (Rogers).

Rogers (2003:186-187) explains reinvention occurs due to a variety of innovation and adopter characteristics. The general reasons include:

- The need to simplify a complex innovation;
- The lack of adopter how-to knowledge (ignorance or inadequate learning);
- The flexibility of the innovation (tightly vs. loosely bundled);
- The broadness of potential applications;
- Status or local pride of ownership;
- Change agency encouragement;
- The need to adapt innovation to fit organizational structure; and
- The point in the diffusion process in which adoption occurs (later adoptions more likely to evidence reinvention)

These rationales demonstrate that the properties of an innovation, and the way it is packaged and presented to a social system, can influence whether the innovation is modified during or following its initial implementation. The concept of reinvention, and particularly the flexibility of the innovation, has special significance to the current investigation as these characteristics and activities help to explain how a legitimate financial opportunity might be transformed for illegitimate use to facilitate a profit from white collar crime.

CHAPTER 5

Applying Diffusion Theory to White Collar Crime

Diffusion theory has provided a rich tradition and framework, guiding hundreds of studies conducted by a wide range of disciplines, across decades of time, with Rogers' original interpretation of the diffusion process remaining relatively consistent over the years (King, 2000; Meyer, 2004). This suggests a number of things, not the least of which is that the diffusion tradition is truly a scientific paradigm as Rogers (2004) suggests (e.g., relevance, questions, methods – see Kuhn, 1996). Most importantly, however, is the fact that it demonstrates the innate flexibility of diffusion models and their widespread applicability to a variety of social and behavioral science investigations, including studies of crime and criminality.

Research in Criminology and Criminal Justice

Over the past sixty years, the breadth of diffusion theory-guided research has been impressive, a fact that Rogers (2004) suggests signifies that it is time for someone to study the "diffusion of diffusion" research! Although diffusion has been a research tradition in at least nine other disciplines, ranging from education, to public health, to geography and regional studies, it has somewhat surprisingly not been well integrated into criminology or criminal justice.

To be sure, as stated previously, the spread of crime and illegal practices have received considerable attention over the years. Many studies have been conducted on problems such as the spread of white collar crime among business elites (Sutherland, 1983), corporate crime (Benson & Cullen, 1998), organizational corruption (Ashforth, Gioia, Robinson & Trevino, 2008), check forgery (Lacoste & Tremblay, 2003), and collective embezzlement in the savings and loan scandal (Pontell & Calavita, 1993). Spatial diffusion studies are also receiving increased attention with respect to crime displacement (Cornish & Clarke, 1987; Eck & Clarke, 2003), homicide patterns (Cohen & Tita, 1999), foreclosure impacts on neighborhood crime rates (Whitworth, 2008), and the diffusion of crime control benefits (Weisburd et al., 2006).

Despite this growing interest in the concept of "diffusion," the application of the fundamental diffusion of innovations perspective to crime and criminal justice issues is rare, and when published the theoretical and empirical implications drawn have not appeared to have generated much interest. A few relevant studies are available, however, and are briefly summarized below.

The historical establishment, abolition, and reestablishment of death penalty policies in the U.S. were examined as innovation in public policy by Mooney and Lee (1999). They were particularly interested in how states (as adopters) modified the comprehensiveness of their policies (as innovations) during three waves of diffusion between 1846 and 1969. They found mixed support for social learning influences across states and across adopter categories (see also Hays, 1996), and for the amount of reinvention occurring at various points in the diffusion process. Mooney and Lee concluded that the type of innovation, social context, and environmental factors may influence the rate of adoption.

Snyder et al. (2009) used diffusion theory to assess the illegal backdating of stock options among CEOs. Their interest was on how legal and illegal innovations diffuse among corporate executives and what communication channels contributed to each type of diffusion. Snyder and colleagues explain that legal innovative business practices diffuse through normal occupational, organizational, and industry channels (see also Coleman, 1987). They contend illegal innovations cannot logically be diffused in similar fashion due to the stealth and opaqueness of crime; individuals cannot learn as vicariously through these channels due to spatial separation, and industry associations do not tend to openly advocate this type of behavior. Snyder et al. found that organizational connections (through shared "board of director" appointments), geographically-proximate social networks, and the opportunity level of the executive within the company (CEO "power") contributed to illegal backdating.

How fraud diffuses via social ties and impersonal communication channels among crime perpetrators and their victims was the subject of a study conducted by Baker and Faulkner (2003). They claim that five factors promote or discourage the diffusion of all types of transactional innovations: product (innovation) attributes; buyer (adopter) attributes and behavior; seller attributes and behavior structure of the social network; and, method of propagation. Using a case study of a gas and oil company that perpetrated intermediate fraud (see Levi, 2008) among its investors, Baker and Faulkner found that the company actually tried to covertly induce a network of diffusion to lure investors into their Ponzi-type scheme (they obviously could not advertise their intentions). They found that the factors associated with the success of the business' intermediate fraud activities (relative influence of the participant/adopter and innovation attributes) were similar to the factors associated with its success when it was operating legally.

Finally, Weiss (1997) and King (2000) used diffusion theory to examine the factors which influence how and why police organizations adopt new policies, tactics and strategies. Weiss surveyed top-level managers in 134 large municipal police departments to assess how risk mediation (aversion to risk), peer emulation, and cosmopolitanism of senior officials influence organizational innovativeness. He found support for each of these influences, but not all effects were direct. For example, risk mediation tended to operate through peer emulation (via knowledge obtained through communication channels), and was conditioned by the size and resources of the department (e.g., large departments are capable of absorbing more risky policies and practices).

King used secondary analysis of The Law Enforcement Management and Administrative Statistics and Police Foundation data to examine the types of innovations encountered by 431 large municipal departments. He demonstrates how innovations can be categorized as radical, technical, programmatic, or administrative, and they include such things as community-oriented policing, affirmative action hiring, and DNA typing. King suggests that innovativeness varies by the type of innovation; for example, innovations which appealed to managers (e.g., AFIS, CAD) were different from those that appealed to line staff (e.g., 9 mm handguns, Tasers), and innovations that enhanced police officer "image" was more readily received and adopted by both.

The examples of criminal justice/criminology research conducted within the diffusion perspective point out that some interest in diffusion of innovations theory has been displayed in the discipline over the past two decades. In combination, these studies demonstrate how the theory can provide a useful framework with which to examine the spread of policy, crime, or victimization across social systems, employing either a historical or contemporary perspective. They also illustrate how social systems or adopters can be defined in a variety of ways, such as states, CEOs, organizations, industries, or investors, and how other elements of the diffusion model (e.g., communication channels, innovations) can be differentially conceptualized and operationalized depending on the nature and needs of the inquiry. These and similar potential benefits of diffusion of innovations theory to the study of white collar crime have been alluded to throughout this study and will now be further explored and illuminated with respect to the specific phenomenon of subprime mortgage fraud in the United States.

With this review of diffusion of innovation and related criminal justice research accomplished, attention now turns to how diffusion of innovations theory is specifically germane to the study of fraud in the subprime mortgage market, the examination and understanding of white collar crime, and the advancement of criminological theory.

Accounting for White Collar Crime

Diffusion theory provides a context capable of interpreting the spread of white collar crimes and the elements, properties, and techniques of white collar crime (see Benson & Simpson, 2009). The theory and its causal models accomplish this in four ways. First, white collar crime can be construed as an illegal innovation or as a reinvention of a legitimate innovation (e.g., see Baker & Faulkner, 2004; Levi, 2008; Snyder et al., 2009). Fraud in the subprime mortgage market is likely attributable to each of these, as it is predicated on access to both opportunities and routines. For example, it is likely that a portion of the fraud can be attributable to individuals and companies which entered the mortgage business precisely to take advantage of the potentially lucrative predatory activities associated with subprime lending. It is also likely that fraud has been committed more often by individuals (and companies) that had been historically engaged in otherwise legitimate mortgage transactions, in what Levi (2008) refers to as *intermediate fraud.* It is anticipated that information from mortgage practitioners will help clarify how both the adoption and reinvention of the subprime mortgage in these respects occurred over time within the industry.

Second, the identified processes and component characteristics of diffusion theory represent why, how, and at what rate, motivation, intentions, opportunity, and techniques are learned, cultivated, and reinforced (e.g., see Haider and Kreps, 2004; or, Pankratz, Hallfors, & Cho, 2002). The five-stage innovation-decision process model (see Figure 4.1) taps into the ways in which individuals become aware of new ideas, characteristics of ideas and information "receivers," and the factors influencing whether or not an innovation is adopted or reinvented. The model also embodies the communication channels through which information travels through a social system, and which, consistent with differential association theory, can tap into the nature of mortgage practitioners' associations and the definitions they ultimately transfer.

Third, the properties of white collar crime (i.e., specialized access, the superficial appearance of legitimacy, and spatial separation from victims) facilitate innovation and reinvention (see Baker & Faulkner, 2003; Benson & Simpson, 2009; Snyder et al., 2009). As has been shown, both the characteristics of the decision-making units and the perceived characteristics of innovations contribute to their adoption, implementation, and reinvention. Similar to what might be modeled with routine activities theory, these components of diffusion theory tap into motivation, target suitability, and guardianship, but the diffusion model further illuminates the process by which these conditions tend to converge under an individual's normal business routines, and how they contribute to an individual's comprehension of potential white collar crime opportunities.

Fourth and finally, white collar crime can be assessed with similar models for individuals and aggregates (see Hays, 1996; Rogers, 2003; Strang & Soule, 1998). Although not covered in detail here, diffusion of innovations theory also includes models designed to investigate and interpret organizational innovativeness and the rate of organizational innovation adoption. For instance, organizational structure and internal and external system characteristics each factor into the innovativeness of an organization (King, 2000; Rogers, 2003; Weiss, 1997). With both individual and aggregate models fully refined under the diffusion perspective, the spread of both occupational and corporate crime can be interpreted. This may prove quite useful in future investigations into the corporate malfeasance associated with subprime mortgage fraud.

In sum, diffusion theory incorporates an extensive array of independent and dependent variables viewed at multiple levels of analysis and across several dimensions (e.g., context, structure, social system, time). In doing so, the theory provides an ideal interpretive and integrative framework for assessing the combination of factors associated with the diffusion of innovation and fraud in the subprime mortgage market in the United States. It has been argued that no one contemporary criminological theory can fully or singlehandedly account for the range of individual, organizational, situational, structural, and contextual factors associated with white collar crime under one conceptual model. It has been demonstrated, however, that diffusion theory, and its developed models, provides a perspective under which a greater variety of factors typically associated with white collar crime (e.g., events, opportunities) and white collar criminality (e.g., motivation, decision-making) can be further and logically interpreted.

Diffusion theory provides an outline for examining and explaining how occupational crime can occur through the adoption or reinvention of financial or other material opportunities (e.g., via the innovation-decision process). Diffusion models can capture individual susceptibility to offend through characteristics of adopters and decision-making units, while attending to structural and contextual factors that may encourage or inhibit offending. Furthermore, the theory also compensates for how motivation and opportunity, undeniably the most critical components of white collar crime (Coleman, 1987), are learned and cultivated though the innovation-diffusion process. It explains the mechanisms responsible for the spread of illegal practices (e.g., through the decision-making process, communication channels) and how the characteristics of a particular type of crime (as an innovation or reinvention) influence the extent and rate of its subsequent diffusion. In combination, the processes, conditions, and characteristics addressed by diffusion of innovations theory suggest the paradigm offers special advancements over traditional criminological theories for the examination and understanding of white collar crime, and can be aptly utilized to examine and interpret subprime mortgage fraud.

CHAPTER 6

Gathering Insights from the Field: Research Strategy

The goal of this study is to investigate how and why legal and illegal practices spread throughout the U.S. mortgage system during the diffusion of subprime lending, and to illustrate how this can best be examined and interpreted under a combination of criminological and non-criminological perspectives. The theoretical argument has already been made: the diffusion of innovations paradigm offers an extension to any one, or combination of, criminological theories in helping to explain how legitimate business opportunities spread and can be transformed or taken advantage of illegitimately.

Consistent with the original definition of diffusion (Rogers, 2003; see Chapter 4) diffusion is defined here as *the process by which subprime lending and subprime fraud have been communicated through certain channels over time among members of the mortgage industry*. The primary factors associated with this diffusion are identified as the *innovation* (i.e., subprime lending; subprime mortgage fraud), *communication channels* (e.g., occupational, organizational, industry contacts; formal or informal), a *social system* (i.e., the mortgage industry) and *time* (see also Haider & Kreps, 2004). The Chapter 2 discussion provided a basic explanation of these factors, and specifically outlined the nature of the innovation (i.e., subprime lending and fraud) and the social system (e.g., the mortgage industry "food chain"). The eight research questions (outlined in Chapter 1) were formulated to extend this discussion and to capture more information on the overall *process* as well as the communication channels and time frame associated with the innovation's diffusion.

The first two questions address the aggregate growth of subprime lending and mortgage fraud over time. The other six are designed to examine mortgage industry practitioners' perspectives on the nature of the use and misuse of subprime lending, how both of these were communicated through the financial community, and what factors contributed to their spread through the mortgage industry over time. The questions were also developed to investigate the opportunity structure of subprime lending, and how the differential associations and routines of mortgage practitioners (e.g., various levels of guardianship) may have facilitated the spread and growth of the white collar crime associated with it.

As can be surmised, the list of research questions represents both an information- and theory-generating agenda, and arguably necessitates a mostly qualitative evaluation. As such, the intent of the methodological approach in this study is designed to augment the previous theoretical discussion of criminological and diffusion theories with descriptive data about the growth rate and extent of subprime lending and fraud, and with information on the diffusion of the innovation and fraud as perceived by practitioners familiar with the intricacies of the housing industry and subprime lending practices.

Ethnography

> *White-collar criminality is found in every occupation, as can be discovered readily in casual conversation with a representative of an occupation by asking him, "what crooked practices are found in your occupation?"* (Sutherland, 1940)

Diffusion of innovations theory has rarely been used in criminological research. In fact, only a handful of studies following the diffusion paradigm were located through an extensive literature search (e.g., Baker & Faulkner, 2003; King, 2000; Mooney & Lee, 1999; Snyder et al., 2009; Weiss, 1997). As such, there was no established diffusion research tradition within criminology to fully emulate for the current investigation. However, of the multidisciplinary diffusion studies that have been reviewed, pre-survey interviews, case studies, surveys, and interviews tended to pre-date any quantitative evaluations in the majority of these investigations (e.g., Baker & Faulkner, 2003; Frame & White, 2009; Pankratz, et al., 2002; Snyder et al., 2009; Trajtenberg & Yitzhaki, 1989; Westphal et al., 1997).

Choosing a qualitative evaluation of white collar crime is consistent with Sutherland's (1940) opening remarks above. To begin to understand the perceptions and beliefs of the members of particular occupations, organizations, and industries, you must first ask the members of these systems themselves (see also Nguyen, 2011). For example, in this project, it is understood there may be distinct influences operating at each stage of the innovation-decision process (i.e., knowledge, persuasion, decision, implementation, confirmation), and different communication channels which contribute to adoption and reinvention. Who better to ask than the individuals who have first-hand knowledge of these influences, processes and channels?

Due to the wide variety of innovations and the potentially unique innovation-decision characteristics associated with them, Rogers (2003:196) suggests that one view any particular process under a dynamic perspective which is capable of explaining the "causes and sequences of a series of events over time." As such, and although he notes this has ramifications for most preferred forms of quantitative analyses, Rogers argues that the more flexible qualitative data collection and process research may be better suited to the task than the more popular variance research. Rogers posits that this type of qualitative research creates a better appreciation of the stages of the innovation-decision process as compared to diffusion variance methodology which tends to focus primarily on the adoption (implementation) stage and rates of adoption. Although adoption rates of subprime lending and fraud have been estimated herein, the focus has remained on the overall process as experienced by the system and its members.

Sample and Research Sites

The sampling technique utilized in this project resulted in a small convenience snowball sample. The invited respondents included targeted and random representatives from the main components of the basic mortgage system (i.e., appraisers, realtors, lenders, brokers, fraud investigators). In June and July 2010, potential respondents were identified through personal networks and through Internet searches of industry-related websites in the Cincinnati/Northern Kentucky, Milwaukee, WI, and Northeastern Wisconsin areas. More potential participants were identified through referrals obtained during the interview process (i.e., participants were asked to supply contact information for other prospective study informants).

Participants were recruited by email, telephone, and through in-person correspondence, and were screened for a current or prior mortgage-related occupation (e.g., as a mortgage service provider, regulator, or fraud investigator) and whether they were so employed during the time of subprime mortgage expansion in the early to mid-1990s or beyond. These criteria were selected as it was anticipated that informants with these characteristics would have knowledge about: the subprime innovation; why and how it diffused throughout the mortgage industry; and, what techniques and rationalizations may have been used to facilitate the use and reinvention of the innovation for illegal purposes.

A total of sixty-three (63) individuals were invited to participate in the study. Of these, 15 agreed to participate (see Table 6.1), 14 reported they felt unqualified (e.g., not in the business long enough) or that the topic was not applicable to their jobs, 5 declined, and 29 did not respond. The fifteen (15) individuals that were interviewed included one appraiser, one realtor, three brokers, eight lenders, and two account executives. Some of these individuals reported employment in a variety of other factions of the real estate or mortgage industry throughout their careers, and their job titles are included as warranted in the results section.

Table 6.1: Sample

Job Title: Organization Type	Years Experience
Account Representative: Mortgage Bank	4
Senior Loan Officer: Brokerage	9
Owner/Manager: Brokerage	10
Account Representative: Mortgage Bank	12
Mortgage Loan Officer: Bank	13
Broker: Independent	16
Manager/Loan Officer: Bank; Former Appraiser	17
Branch Manager: Bank & Trust	19
Realtor: Realty	23
Senior Mortgage Consultant: Savings & Loan	26
Retail Sales Manager: Bank	27
Commercial Loan Officer: Bank & Trust	27
Loan Officer: Bank & Trust	30
Mortgage Loan Specialist: Bank	35
President: Savings & Loan	38

The respondents had a range of experience from 4 to 38 years, with a median time in the business of 19 years, and an average of 20.4 years. The geographic composition of the sample included three participants from Northeastern Wisconsin, three from the Milwaukee, Wisconsin area, two from Florida, and the remaining seven from the greater Cincinnati, Ohio metropolitan area.

Data Collection and Processing

The research strategy of this project was comprised of two primary components: (1) assessing the spread of subprime lending and reported mortgage fraud throughout the U. S. mortgage lending industry over time; and, (2) investigating mortgage industry professionals' perceptions of the nature of the subprime mortgage, the fraud associated with it, the process by which both of these diffused throughout the financial industry over time, and how individuals seized the opportunity to participate in them.[24] As noted above, these elements are consistent with the four diffusion factors (an innovation, communication channels, a social system, and time) identified by Rogers (2003) and Haider & Kreps (2004). Although quantitative analysis was not employed, these study *parameters* are consistent with the majority of those examined in the diffusion research (Trajtenberg & Yitzhaki, 1989).

The first task associated with the research strategy centered on an assessment of the growth of subprime lending throughout the U.S. financial industry over time, and was accomplished via a review of

---

[24] IRB and Informed Consent: The Institutional Review Board (IRB) of a University requires that all social and behavioral research carried out at the University involving human subjects must be approved prior to the undertaking of any research activities. IRB approval was received for this project on April 5, 2010. The IRB review and approval process is intended to promote ethical conduct and to ensure that the subjects and other information and processes (e.g., data; data collection and processing) are treated with integrity, including that all subjects understand their rights and the risks and rewards of participating in the research. This understanding was conveyed in the current study through an informed consent document which explained the project, such as the purpose of the study, requirements for participation, a statement of potential risks and benefits to participants, and the like. Each participant was required to acknowledge understanding of these by signing the document prior to being interviewed.

public-access data.[25] Various government-sponsored agencies and sources, including FinCEN and the Department of Housing and Urban Development (HUD), were reviewed for aggregate national, regional, state, and MSA longitudinal and cross-sectional loan and lender information (as posted on their respective websites with publicly accessible data). This component of the examination provided a descriptive account of the extent of subprime lending and loan volumes over time (i.e., innovation-diffusion), and inadvertently demonstrates how a particular opportunity for white collar crime spread through a specific social system. As stated previously, it was anticipated that consistent with prior diffusion research the subprime innovation rate of adoption would follow the classic S-curve distribution.

The next task was to locate and review public-access data (for example, from the FBI, SEC, Department of the Treasury, etc.) regarding the extent of reported mortgage fraud in the subprime market. This element of the examination was intended to demonstrate the growth rate of subprime mortgage fraud allegations and investigations over time (i.e., the innovation reinvention). In comparing the rates and the nature of their growth (lending and fraud allegations), the extent of the fraud committed through the adoption and/or reinvention of subprime lending tools and techniques is illuminated. It was further anticipated that this aspect of the study would demonstrate a geographic clustering of fraud within certain market territories, suggesting that interpersonal social networking and other spatial and contextual conditions may contribute to the spread of illegal behaviors. Although not investigated directly herein, this may be consistent with the importance of more informal (local) communication channels to the adoption of illegal over legal innovations (e.g., see Snyder et al., 2009).

The third task of the data collection consisted of scheduling, performing, and recording in-depth interviews with a number of professionals currently or previously involved in the mortgage industry

---

[25] Data and estimates on subprime lending and fraud were updated for this monograph.

(e.g., appraisers, brokers, lenders). The interview process was conducted during June and July of 2010. Participants were asked to submit to a semi-structured interview (in person or by phone) with the investigator to shed light on the research questions and to share their professional and personal perceptions and opinions, for example, about subprime lending and fraud. A series of interview questions and a variety of prompts were devised to assist the researcher in stimulating conversation with the participants (see Appendix A: Interview Guide).

The specific questions and prompts were designed to tap into the fundamental elements of the subprime industry, the history of the subprime innovation diffusion, and fraud. The areas of interest underlying the questions included participant job status, origins and characteristics of subprime lending, communication channels, subprime fraud, industry regulation, and the general stages of the innovation-decision process (see Figure 4.1). For instance, a question about the origins of subprime lending was designed to assess prior conditions and knowledge, whereas a question about the subprime characteristics that may have made it more amenable to fraud than other lending tools was designed to tap into the strength of persuasion. The interview prompts further address the elements which combine to represent these stages, as well as reinvention and fraud. For example, questions were designed to investigate perceptions about the core elements of the innovation, how/why the elements could be altered, and how individuals may have learned of this potential.

Similarly, the fraud questions were designed to capture the practitioners' understandings of how fraud may have been perceived as being relatively advantageous, compatible with legitimate operations, and easy to try and partake in by industry professionals. It should be noted that respondents were never asked about their own potentially illegal behavior or participation in criminal activity. Participants were also asked to supply any industry-related policy documents or publications that they believed would be useful in illustrating the techniques and tools of the subprime mortgage trade.

The ½- to 1-hour interviews were conducted at the business headquarters of the respective informants (n=12), at an agreeable neutral location (n=2) or by phone (n=1). This latter aspect of the interviewing, phone interviews, allowed for the recruitment of potential participants outside of the previously identified geographic areas, such as in the Southern Florida area. Although respondents had the option to not have the interview recorded, all participants agreed, and each of the interviews was digitally recorded to facilitate a complete transcription of each contact. The interviews resulted in approximately 14 hours of digital recordings and 200 pages of single-spaced transcripts. The qualitative data analysis software, NVivo[26] (QSR International, 2010), was then utilized to assess the interview transcripts by organizing and structuring their contents among a variety of themes and criminological and diffusion keywords, such as communication channels, learning, opportunity, culture, trickery, greed, collusion, competition, and events of the 1990s and early-2000s.

In sum, it was anticipated that the practitioner interview element of the research would: (1) help to make sense of the literature and public-access data; and, (2) equip the investigator with a more thorough understanding of which perceived characteristics of the subprime innovation help to explain its historical rate of adoption, the stages of the innovation-decision process, and the qualities of the subprime mortgage itself which may have enabled adopters to embrace or reinvent it for illicit gains. In reporting the perceptions of the participants (e.g., general themes and individual beliefs about critical issues), it will also help to illuminate factors and concerns that may not have been addressed in the literature but which may be integral to further research in this area.

---

[26] QSR International (2010) claims: "Qualitative research is all about exploring issues, understanding phenomena and answering questions. It happens in nearly every workplace, it's just you might not know it by its formal name. Qualitative research uses unstructured information – like field notes, videos, transcripts and audio recordings, instead of numbers to arrive at conclusions. Our software lets you manage, shape and make sense of this information quickly and easily."

Summary and Limitations

It was well-understood at the outset of this study that the ethnographic aspect of this research conducted via the above means would not lend itself well to quantitative analysis. Due to the descriptive nature of the public-access data, the small purposive and unrepresentative sample (with no representation from the secondary market), and the poor response rate, it also has minimal external validity and lacks generalizability. The results also lack a marked degree of internal validity with respect to a number of factors. The fraud revealed in the subprime market may be due to unmeasured or unconsidered factors unassociated with aspects of the specific innovation itself or its subsequent diffusion (e.g., technology). These historical and potentially confounding relationship factors have hopefully been identified, or at least marginally illuminated, by the project informants.

What the qualitative evaluation has provided, however, is a description of the perceptions, attitudes, and understandings of the individuals who are most intimate with subprime lending, how the idea was presented to and diffused by the mortgage industry over time, and how the innovation and occupational routines were eventually used to facilitate the commission of white collar crime. This information helps to clarify the nature of the mortgage system, the types of communication channels operating within the system, and how these various channels or associations may have promoted the legitimate *and* illegitimate applications of subprime mortgage tools. All told, this qualitative research design follows the advice of Sutherland (1983) and Rogers (2003) and is consistent with the type of qualitative process evaluation[27] needed to promote eventual theory building with regard to the diffusion of innovation/white collar crime relationship.

---

[27] This detailed interview methodology is also consistent with Clarke's (1999:9) interpretation of "action research" with respect to investigating "situational conditions that permit or facilitate" a narrowly defined crime such as subprime mortgage fraud (see also e.g., Posavac & Carey, 2007; Rossi, Lipsey & Freeman, 2004).

CHAPTER 7

Subprime Lending and Mortgage Fraud Diffusion

> *It sounds complicated, but it's really fairly simple: banks lent hundreds of billions of dollars to homebuyers who can't pay them back. Wall Street took the risky debt, dressed it up as fancy securities, and sold it around the world as safe investments. If it sounds like a shell game or Ponzi scheme, in some ways it was a house of cards rife with corruption, greed, and negligence* (CBS, 2008).

The factors that contributed to the subprime mortgage crisis have been referred to as the building blocks of a "house of cards" (CBS, 2008) that was eventually doomed to fall. It may be easy to identify these causes in retrospect, but the process by which this combination of factors was developed and enabled to spread, and coexist, has not been well established. The following discussion is intended to extend this understanding and bring more meaning to the subprime mortgage crisis by clarifying the characteristics of the products and individuals which facilitated and added to it.

This chapter is organized around the first two of the eight research questions set forth in Chapter 1. The first question addresses the diffusion of subprime lending, and the second focuses on the diffusion of mortgage fraud reported over time. The descriptive data and the discussion of the nature and extent of these diffusions supplements and expands the prior subprime and mortgage industry discussion in Chapter 2.

Diffusion of Subprime Lending

> **Research Question #1**: *What has been the rate and extent of the diffusion of subprime lending and has this been consistent with the S-curve distribution notable in the classic diffusion model (Rogers, 2003)?*

The first research question is designed to examine the spread of subprime mortgage lending since the practice became more legitimized during the 1990s. Using public-access information and data, it is shown below that although subprime lending initially comprised only a small proportion of total mortgage originations (loans) in the 1990s, it escalated into a formidable component of the mortgage market and the global economy by the early 2000s.

As expected from the definitional issues of "subprime" as outlined in Chapter 2, Mayer and Pence (2008:1) demonstrate that "estimates of the number of subprime originations are somewhat sensitive to which types of mortgages are categorized as subprime." For example, they suggest:

> The LP [LoanPerformance][28] measure implies that subprime originations grew seven-fold from 1998 to 2005, whereas the

---

[28] "LoanPerformance (LP) are loans that were packaged into subprime mortgage pools" (Mayer & Pence, 2008:21) and are defined as "mortgages in securitized pools marketed as subprime by the securitizer" (p. 1). "The

> HMDA HUD measure implies that originations tripled over this period. The difference between the two measures appears to stem from growth in subprime securitization over these years. If we restrict the HUD measure to originations that were securitized, the two series track each other closely in most years. These findings suggest that which measure captures the subprime market best may vary as the market structure evolves over time (Mayer and Pence, 2008:2).

As Mayer and Pence note, estimates of the extent of subprime lending over time vary according to source. Figure 7.1 illustrates that of the total number of subprime mortgages pooled into securities, subprime refinances (LP REFI) had steady growth from 2000 and 2005, and subprime purchase originations (LP PURCHASE) had slower but increasing growth from 2002 to 2005.

---

data do not include mortgages held in portfolio, securitized mortgages in prime, jumbo, or AltA pools, or loans guaranteed by government agencies such as the Federal Housing Administration and the Veterans' Administration or by government sponsored enterprises such as Fannie Mae, Freddie Mac or Ginnie Mae. The data also exclude loans securitized by lenders that do not report to LoanPerformance. Comparing the LP subprime totals to the subprime MBS totals published by Inside Mortgage Finance (Inside Mortgage Finance, 2006) suggests that LP captures around 90 percent of the subprime securitized market from 1999 to 2002 and nearly all of the market from 2003 to 2005" (Mayer & Pence, p. 3). HMDA is the Home Mortgage Disclosure Act, and HUD is the United States Department of Housing and Urban Development. Mayer and Pence (p. 1) define HMDA HUD loans as those "mortgages originated by lenders specializing in subprime mortgages."

Figure 7.1: Subprime Originations by Year: LoanPerformance (LP)* Definition

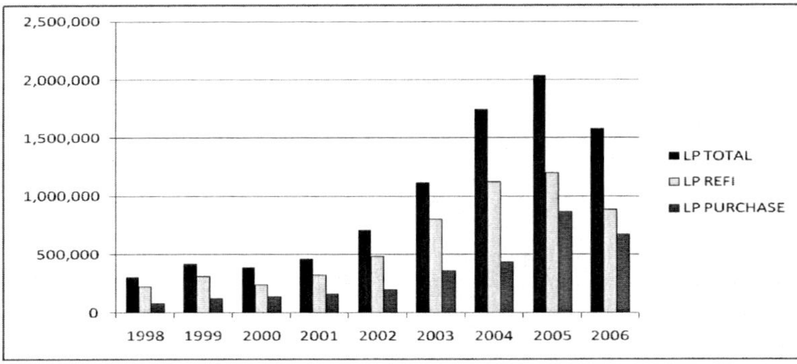

*LoanPerformance (LP) are loans that were packaged into subprime mortgage pools. LP REFI indicates refinance loans, and LP PURCHASE indicates home purchase loans. Source: Adapted from Mayer and Pence (2008:21).

Figure 7.2: Subprime Originations by Year: HMDA HUD Subprime Lenders

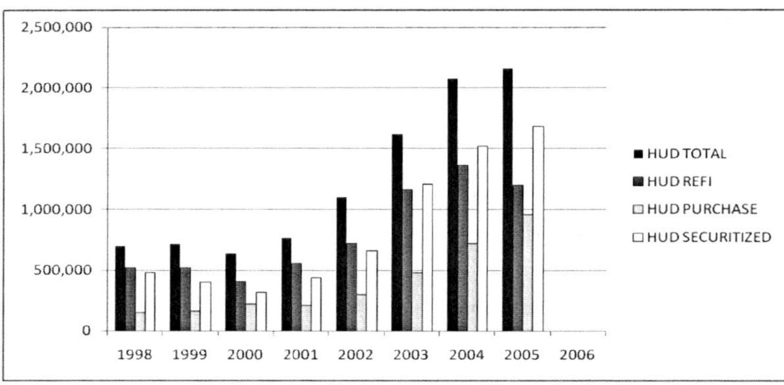

Source: Adapted from Mayer and Pence (2008:21).

Similarly, Figure 7.2 illustrates the number of loans recorded as being originated by HUD lenders which specialized in subprime mortgages from 1998 through 2005, and offers a breakdown of the total loans, refinances, purchases, and those packaged for securities. As illustrated, mortgage refinances consistently outranked purchases, but by 2005 the volume of purchase originations were almost on pace with refinances (but still made up a lower percentage of the total subprime HUD lender originations). These differences will be elaborated on in the discussion of research question #5 in Chapter 8. Other sources report even greater volume increases. For example, Gramlich (2007:1) indicates "subprime mortgage originations were a mere $35 billion in 1994, less than 5 percent of total mortgage originations. By 2005, subprime originations had risen to $625 billion ... now up to 20 percent of total originations and 7 percent of the total outstanding mortgage stock. Over the decade, subprime originations increased 17-fold, a whopping 26 percent annual rate of increase." And finally, Chomsisengphet and Pennington-Cross (2006) estimated that subprime originations (also based on securitizations), grew over five times between 1995 and 2003, as shown in Figure 7.3.

Figure 7.3: Subprime (B&C*) Growth Curve**

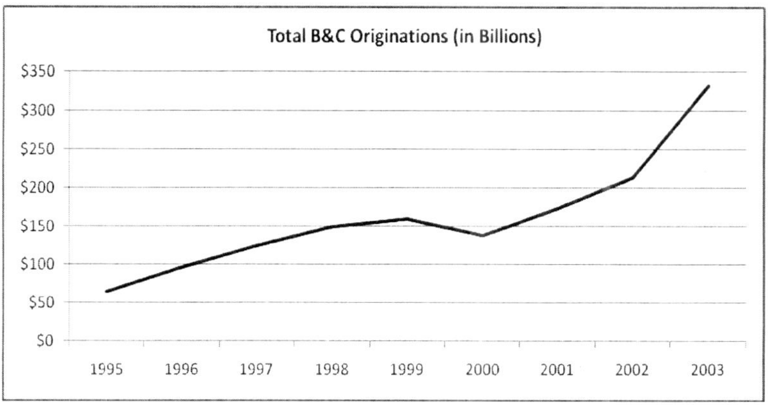

*Subprime is referred to here as B&C (e.g., less than A-rated loans). Source: Adapted from *Inside B&C Lending* as cited in Chomsisengphet and Pennington-Cross (2006:37).

**Based on Data in Table 2.1.

Despite the wide range of estimates of the volume of subprime loan originations since the mid-90s, one thing is certain: what began as a small portion of mortgage lending activity became a significant factor in the industry within a relatively short period of time. Each of the estimates reveal that subprime originations held a steadily increasing pace throughout the end of the 90s, took a dip in 2000, and then escalated from 2001 forward.

Figure 7.4: Diffusion Curve[29] of Subprime Mortgaging*

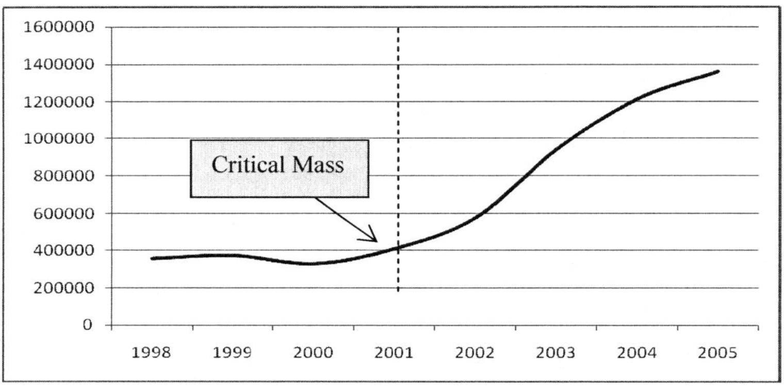

*Average of LP and HMDA HUD Subprime Lenders Originations. Adapted from Mayer and Pence (2008).

From a diffusion of innovations perspective, the turning point in 2001 (estimated with the dashed vertical line in Figure 7.4) is approximately the time period in the diffusion process in which enough individuals in the mortgage industry had adopted subprime lending to

---

[29] As the actual number of lenders or "individual adopters" of the subprime mortgage over time is ambiguous and unobtainable through readily available public data, the volume of subprime originations is being used as a proxy to illustrate the rate of adoption of the subprime innovation. This factor also restricts the ability to estimate a cumulative "adoption curve" (see Figure 4.3).

enable the tool to become self-sustaining. After this time, the level of subprime originating did not dip below prior levels, and only moved in an upward direction. Rogers (2003) refers to this as the time at which "critical mass" is achieved; prior to reaching critical mass, the rate of adoption is slow, but once this point is reached, the rate of adoption accelerates. In sum, the spread of subprime lending, as demonstrated by its growth from the mid-1990s to the mid-2000s, is estimated to have followed the classic S-curve adoption trend noted in a vast majority of diffusion studies.

Diffusion of Subprime Fraud

> **Research Question #2**: *What has been the rate and extent of the diffusion of fraud in the subprime market?*

Similar to the first research question, public-access information and descriptive data are used here to address the second question, which is intended to capture the growth and distribution of subprime mortgage fraud. As indicated previously, during the height of the growth in subprime lending in the late-1990s/early-2000s, another phenomenon was also diffusing rapidly throughout the U.S. financial sector, that being mortgage fraud. Although the true extent and total damages related to mortgage fraud (which has always existed to some extent), and in particular the frauds associated with subprime lending, are not readily identifiable, there are nonetheless indicators which can be used to at least estimate its diffusion and growth, such as the Suspicious Activity Report (SAR) filings to U.S. regulatory and law enforcement agencies.

SARs are reports that are completed by financial institutions whenever a transaction is suspected of being fraudulent or to cover up some other type of illegal activity, and are forwarded to the Financial Crimes Enforcement (FinCEN) section of the Department of the Treasury for potential investigation. This illegal activity includes everything from money laundering to identity theft. The information contained within the reports also provides cursory information that is relevant here. For example, "between 1997 and 2004, SARs filed by

Figure 7.5: Comparison of Increases in Mortgage Loan Fraud SARs to All Other SARs[30]

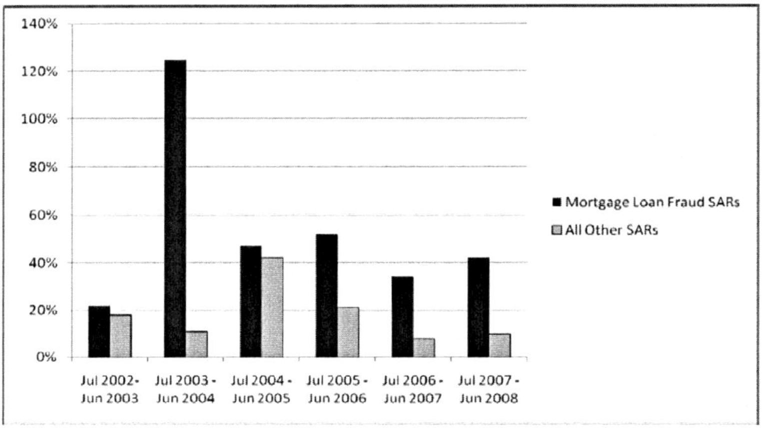

Source: Adapted from FinCEN (2009b:9).

depository institutions reporting mortgage loan fraud increased by 969 percent" (FinCEN, 2006b:13),[31] with a one-year explosion of a 126% increase in mortgage loan fraud SARs from July 2003 through June 2004 alone. Figure 7.5 illustrates the annual percentage increases in

---

30 Filing volumes reflect reporting and increases may not be indicative of fraudulent activities occurring during within the specified time period (FinCEN, 2012:2).

31 "The total dollar amount of suspicious activity reported for the period between April 1, 1996 and June 30, 2005 was $16,748,111,493. In July 2005, the national median price for existing homes for all housing types was $218,000, according to the National Association of Realtors. Over 58 percent of the mortgage loan fraud reports fell into the range between $100,001 and $500,000. Seven of the top ten SAR filers in this study reporting mortgage loan fraud also were listed in the top three percent of 1,506 nationally ranked U.S.-chartered commercial banks with consolidated assets of $300 million or more. However, this could be due to their market share in mortgage lending" (FinCEN, 2006b:14).

SARs reports to FinCEN by fiscal year. For example, in FY '06-'07, mortgage fraud SARs increased by over 30% whereas all other SARs combined for less than a 10% increase over FY '05-'06.

Similar to the origination and lender data, fraud figures are also difficult to assess as they are continually being updated. As such, SARs can only be used as a *proxy* for the diffusion of fraud associated with the subprime mortgage market. As noted by FinCEN (2009b:10), by 2008, "the growth rate of mortgage loan fraud SARs outpaced that of all other SARs over each of the past 6 annual periods, often by a considerable amount." As demonstrated in Figure 7.5, even though other types of fraud (e.g., credit card or identity theft) reported under SARs also showed annual increases between 2002 and 2008, the extent of their respective SARs increases was only comparable to mortgage fraud reports in two of these fiscal years (FY '02-'03 and FY '04-'05).

Figure 7.6: Mortgage Loan Fraud SARs: 1997-2009

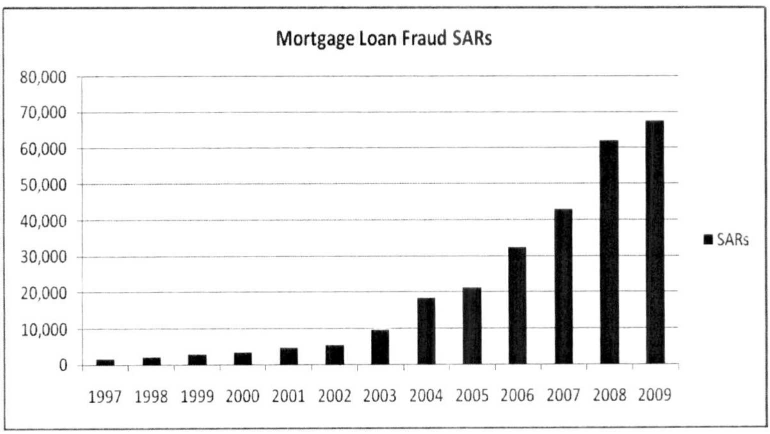

Source: Adapted from FinCEN (2006b:14; 2009b:7&8; 2010:5).

Figure 7.6 illustrates the exponential growth in mortgage fraud reporting in the years from 1997 through 2009. As shown, SARs doubled between 2002 and 2003, and again between 2003 and the middle of 2004, and have continued to increase annually since 1997. In 2010, mortgage loan fraud SARs exceeded 70,500 (FBI, 2011:13). FinCEN (2010:4) cautions, however, that the annual increases "are not entirely reflective of fraud activity. SAR submissions are currently only required of federally-insured financial institutions and their affiliates." Nevertheless, both FinCEN and the FBI (2010) rely on the SARs data to estimate the level of fraud occurring on an annual basis.

Even if one disagrees that the "reporting" of fraud cannot be a proxy for the actual fraud occurrences, SARs arguably represent the industry's best guess as to the extent of fraud being committed on an annual basis.[32] One must concede that SARs may also at least minimally reflect the industry's attention to the problem of fraud within its economic institutions, as SARs represent mandated, yet unsolicited, descriptions of possible fraudulent transactions which threaten the financial security of the nation's financial system.

As demonstrated in Figure 7.7, the critical mass in the growth of fraud reporting (estimated in early-2003 and noted by the vertical dashed line in Figure 7.7) occurred roughly two years after the point at which critical mass was achieved in subprime loan originations (Figure 7.4). This is the approximate point at which all prior fraud reporting levels were surpassed and in which no annual level to date has been lower than the year directly preceding it.

As will be explained in more detail below, this time of critical mass is not an anomaly, rather it is approximately the point at which the initial high volume wave of adjustable rate subprime mortgages (ARMs) began to "adjust" and loan defaults began to accrue. As investigators (e.g., internal and external auditors, regulators, etc.) began to explore the details of these loans and their original mortgage transactions, fraudulent activities began to be uncovered at an alarming

---

[32] This is arguably parallel to the use of the Uniform Crime Reports to estimate crime rates based on crimes known to law enforcement, although there is no complementary reporting system, such as the National Victimization Survey or National Incident Based Reporting System, to even make adequate comparisons.

rate, attention to fraud increased, and SARs subsequently began to escalate at exceptional speed.

Figure 7.7: Diffusion Curve of Subprime Mortgage Loan Fraud SARs*

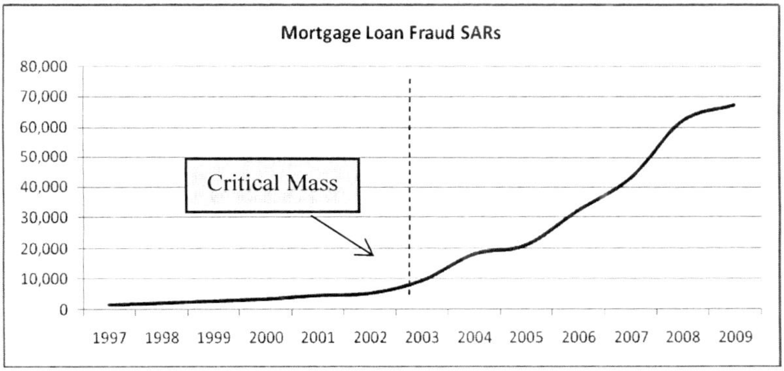

*Filings by depository institutions. Source: Adapted from FinCEN (2006b:14; 2009b:7&8; 2010:5).

In addition to fraud reporting indicators, the types and geographic distribution of reported mortgage fraud is also captured in data collected from various national sources. For example, Fannie Mae disentangles fraudulent activity in the loans delivered to its agency along eight dimensions. Table 7.1 illustrates a multi-year distribution of these types of material misrepresentations.

Although the percentages noted in Table 7.1 reflect the portion of specific misrepresentations on all types of fraud related to mortgage loans (subprime is not disentangled), it does highlight that different types of fraud are being detected as more prevalent in some years over others. For example, note that false statements of borrower liabilities and income declined in 2009, but have consistently been the top forms of fraud. The buyer's intent to occupy the property (e.g., primary residence vs. investment property) was misrepresented more often in the 2010 loan originations than in the prior two years, and the level of asset misrepresentations also rose dramatically between 2008 and 2009.

Property "value" misrepresentations fell sharply by 2010, and finally, credit and social security number (SSN) misrepresentations varied little during this time, but as is shown each of these still make up a lower proportion of the total fraud reported.

Table 7.1: Annual Percentage of Misrepresentations by Type[33]

Type	2008	2009	2010	2011/2012
Credit	3	4	3	2
SSN	4	6	6	7
Liabilities	27	24	25	42
Value	6	4	2	4
Property	17	17	14	12
Assets	3	6	7	1
Income	26	21	24	16
Occupancy	14	18	19	16

*Value reflects the percentage of each misrepresentation type out of the total suspect loans delivered to Fannie Mae; as fraudulent loans may include more than one type of misrepresentation, totals may not equal 100%.
Source: Adapted from Fannie Mae (2009-2012).

---

33 "**Credit**: The borrower's identity and/or credit history was/were misrepresented. **SSN**: There is a significant discrepancy in the SSN(s) used to qualify the borrower(s). **Liabilities**: The borrower's liabilities were misrepresented. **Value**: The property value was inflated and there was non-property-related misrepresentation in the loan transaction. **Property**: A specific material fact about the property and/or the comparable sales was misrepresented. **Assets**: The borrower's asset information was inflated or fabricated. **Income**: The borrower's income/employment information was inflated or fabricated. **Occupancy**: The borrower's intent to occupy the subject property was materially misrepresented" (Fannie Mae, 2012).

All told, these figures suggest that increased attention to certain types of misrepresentations of more readily verifiable representations following the subprime crisis, for example on income, value and property as compared to liabilities, may be acting as a deterrent to these specific types of fraud.

Table 7.2: Mortgage Fraud Index Rank by State on Subprime Originations: 2001-2005

State	2001	2002	2003	2004	2005
Florida	9	3	2	1	1
Utah	3	6	3	3	2
Missouri	11	20	12	26	3
Illinois	6	9	14	15	4
Georgia	2	1	1	2	5
Colorado	18	16	6	4	6
Texas	27	12	11	9	7
Rhode Island	33	8	41	37	8
Arkansas	40	41	4	30	9
Ohio	8	15	19	16	10
***	**	**	**	**	**
So. Carolina	1	2	13	12	22

Source: Adapted from Mortgage Asset Research Institute (2006).

Fannie Mae (2009-2012) also publishes an annual display of the geographic distribution of the volume of fraud detected within loans it has subsidized from states and regions of the United States. Of special note has been the rise in the percentage of detected misrepresentations in the Northeast between 2007 (8% of fraud reports) and 2009 (20% of fraud reports), while the Southeast fell by similar percentages (32% to

20%) during this time. With the exception of California, which varied from 14% in 2008 to 31% in 2010, the other regions remained relatively stable in their respective contributions to the total amount of reported fraud. This jockeying among the regions is attributable to both the volume of originations and amount of fraud detected within their respective states. Individual state activity is reflected in their "Mortgage Fraud Index" ranks, which are based on subprime originations (see Table 7.2) and overall loan originations (see Table 7.3) as determined by the Mortgage Asset Research Institute (MARI). These time frames are reported separately as fraud associated with subprime originations were only distinguished into 2005.

Furthermore, as shown in Table 7.3, MARI breaks the level of misrepresentations down by state over time, including the change in fraud index rank for the currently top-ranked states. Also reported in Table 7.3 are the actual Mortgage Fraud Index scores (MFI) that MARI calculates. An MFI score of 100 indicates the state had precisely the volume of reported fraud expected based on the number of residential mortgages it originated (it is the historical baseline) and a score of 0 would mean no fraud was detected. In 2010, Florida ranked highest on the MFI for the fifth year in a row with an MFI of 302. MARI (2011:6) explains that this MFI "indicates that the state has just over three times the expected amount of reported mortgage fraud for its origination volume."

MARI (2009) provides evidence that MFI scores and state ranks are dependent on loan type (e.g. subprime; any), and continue to vacillate, with the caveat that increased (or decreased) state and federal regulatory and investigative priorities are certainly factors to be considered as potential influences on these macro-level fraud estimates.

For example, on *all* originations (Table 7.3), Florida, California and Michigan maintained top ten ranks from 2005 through 2010, while Florida, Utah and Georgia ranked within the top ten *subprime* fraud index states between 2001 and 2005 (Table 7.2). These ranks and rates continually fluctuate as a greater percentage of SARs are reviewed and

Table 7.3: Rank and Mortgage Fraud Index (MFI) by State on All Originations: 2005-2010

State	2010	2009	2008	2007	2006	2005
	Rank *(MFI)*	**Rank** *(MFI)*	**Rank** *(MFI)*	**Rank** *(MFI)*	**Rank** *(MFI)*	**Rank** *(MFI)*
Florida	**1** *(302)*	**1** *(361)*	**1** *(445)*	**1** (372)	**1** (230)	**3** (184)
New York	**2** *(279)*	**3** *(262)*	**5** *(162)*	**21** *(52)*	**12** *(79)*	**11** *(100)*
California	**3** *(233)*	**10** *(130)*	**7** *(156)*	**4** *(152)*	**2** *(166)*	**8** *(119)*
New Jersey	**4** *(191)*	**5** *(155)*	**11** *(107)*	**19** *(57)*	**19** *(56)*	**18** *(65)*
Maryland	**5** *(163)*	**8** *(152)*	**4** *(171)*	**13** *(67)*	**15** *(66)*	**28** *(45)*
Michigan	**6** *(130)*	**6** *(155)*	**3** *(182)*	**3** *(186)*	**4** *(160)*	**2** *(196)*
Virginia	**7** *(113)*	**23** *(79)*	**20** *(53)*	**11** *(75)*	**13** *(71)*	**24** *(49)*
Ohio	**8** *(112)*	**24** *(78)*	**29** *(37)*	**26** *(46)*	**14** *(70)*	**
Colorado	**9** *(96)*	**32** *(50)*	**17** *(61)*	**16** *(62)*	**9** *(106)*	**
Illinois	**10** *(93)*	**11** *(126)*	**8** *(154)*	**7** *(130)*	**6** *(125)*	**5** *(146)*

Source: Adapted from Mortgage Asset Research Institute (MARI, 2010; 2011).

**Missing data.

loans are audited.[34] For example, in a 2009 MARI Report, Rhode Island was reported as having little detected fraud in 2004, with a MFI of 16 and a state rank of 41; by 2008, the state was identified as number 1 on the MFI with a score of 315. In the 2005-2010 report data reported in Table 7.3, Rhode Island is not even reflected in the data, and was replaced by Florida with the highest recorded MFI in 2008.

Summary

In sum, the public-access data available for estimating fraud in the subprime mortgage market provides a limited account of the growth and extent of illegal behavior that has been occurring within the housing industry over the past decade. It does show, however, that the *detection* of fraud escalated dramatically from 2003 forward, approximately two years following the acceleration of subprime lending.[35] Despite the current limitations on lending to under-qualified borrowers, a number of states continue to detect excessive amounts of fraud with respect to the volume of mortgage transactions being originated within their boundaries on an annual basis, a condition that cannot be explained by a simple review of the historical data (FBI, 2010). This will also require further investigation beyond this study.

Due to the evolving, vague and oftentimes indistinct quality of the information available and examined, loan origination and SARs reports from various sources were used herein to proxy subprime lending and fraud. In consideration of the above, however, it can be demonstrated that subprime lending diffused through the U.S. mortgage industry beginning in the mid-1990s, lending reached critical mass around 2001, and the diffusion virtually ended in 2007. It was also illustrated that

---

[34] Although outside of the scope of the current study, this also might suggest either consistently more fraud or consistently higher investigative and regulatory activity within various states over time.

[35] This also suggests that estimates of white collar crime in general are correlated with reports of its extent, and further highlights that a limitation of the data is it cannot account for the "true" or "dark figure" of mortgage fraud.

subprime fraud similarly diffused, reached critical mass around 2003, and that it is evolving into different forms and practices to this day (i.e., there are no limits to innovation and reinvention).

CHAPTER 8

Innovation and Reinvention

To begin to understand the progression and the eventual demise of subprime lending, interviews with participants in the mortgage lending industry were used to address the third and subsequent research questions. The perceptions of mortgage practitioners give an insider's view on subprime lending … from the good and the bad, to the ugly.

Knowledge of Innovations

> **Research Question #3**: *Do knowledge of innovations and their potential reinventions (legal or illegal) diffuse simultaneously or is there a lag between the innovation and the reinvention diffusions?*

While Figures 7.4 and 7.7 in the previous chapter illustrated the growth of subprime lending, that it began escalating around 2001, and that it preceded the acceleration of subprime fraud reporting (as a proxy for subprime fraud) by two years, the public-access data cannot explain why or how this process unfolded. The current question was developed to assess when mortgage practitioners first learned about subprime lending (i.e., the innovation), and when they learned about the types of fraud (i.e., as innovations or reinventions) that were being attributed to it, and what factors contributed to this knowledge.

The research respondents report that the timing of the original escalation is correlated with the legislative and regulatory actions of the mid-90s which eased credit restrictions and encouraged lending to historically under-qualified home buyers. The timeliness of the critical mass point appears correlated with the post-9/11 attempts to stabilize the temporarily stagnant and struggling economy, as well as the increased demand for mortgage-backed securities in the secondary global financial markets. As one broker contends:

> My take on it is, 2001, a couple of guys decided to fly some planes into the towers; the United States was on the verge of an economic meltdown. In order to avoid that, you had to do something – so, the American Dream – everybody gets a house. I think the onset of subprime mortgages saved us from an economic meltdown back then, but it turns out it only prolonged it.

One account executive summarizes the rise of subprime lending from the consumer's perspective:

> … in the early-2000s, everything was rosy, people had tons of equity, they were able to cash out, pay off credit cards, you know take that vacation that they wanted, pay off, you know it was cheaper to buy a car for cash and take the interest as a tax deduction than it was to go finance a car. So there were benefits to taking the cash out of your properties, assuming that, you know, no one foresaw that the property values were going to collapse.

And the end of subprime lending as it was known came to an abrupt halt in 2007. Although two respondents indicated that it was a slow death, others argue the end came virtually overnight:

> ... they didn't tighten things up with subprime, subprime was just *gone*. They didn't, it's not like right now where they're making changes to lending guidelines every, every day. They didn't analyze it. They didn't go "where are the problems here?" – they just *took it out*. It was just done. In like a weekend. It was crazy ... they all got together and made decisions and said "we're going to stop subprime lending altogether" (Brokerage Owner/Manager).

It appears that as soon as the larger traditional banks put an end to their purchasing of subprime loans for the secondary markets, smaller firms followed suit quite quickly and the market was virtually shut down. Based on the information from the interviewees and the data gathered from public sources, a timeline of the subprime lifespan can be illustrated as follows in Figure 8.10:

Figure 8.1: Timeline of the Subprime Diffusion

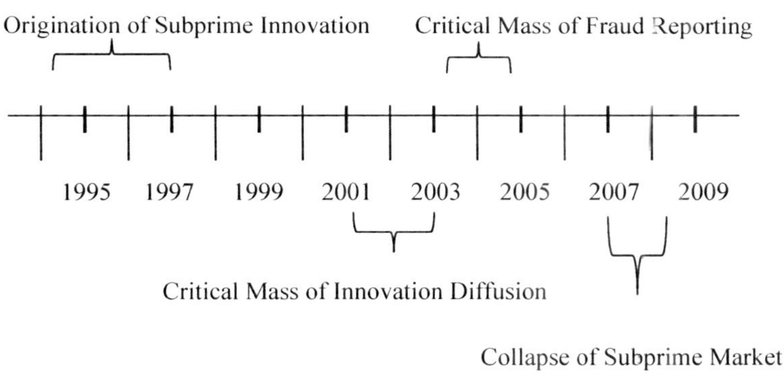

The timeline represents when practitioners became generally aware of subprime lending and fraud. The concern reflected in Question #3, however, is with how and when they specifically learned (on an applied or practical basis) about the legitimate and illegitimate applications of subprime lending – that is, at the same time or at different times?

Approximately 50% of the practitioners agreed that they first learned about the various subprime products (e.g., pay-option ARMs, low or no documentation, stated income) on an individual basis throughout 1990s to early 2000s from the subprime lender account executives or account "reps" who would solicit business from brokers, lenders, realtors, originators, and the like. For many organizations, the reps would not only "cold-call," but would also, according to one broker, often arrange luncheons in which they would explain the details of the various products they had to offer. Furthermore, one lender indicated that the companies offering the subprime products advertised extensively on television, radio, billboards, and other media, so there was a parallel *consumer* knowledge base developing during this time as well.

In sum, the mortgage and financial industries were being educated about the subprime innovation at the same time the general public was learning about it. This knowledge escalated to the point at which potential borrowers would approach their normal (traditional; savings & loans) banks with financing requests. For example, one lender claims:

> There was pressure on even the regular community banks to do this [subprime] because people would call up that perhaps were your customers, "well I've seen this advertised with so-and-so, no down payment, no this, if you're self-employed come, if you've got 20% down and a decent credit score, then you have no documentation" ... it could be anything from signs on telephone poles that say "no down payment, call," "we sell to renters" ... but I don't think they were told everything that it would take necessarily to succeed and certainly what the ultimate costs would be in terms of principal, interest, taxes, and insurance.

This lender further explained that customers may have regularly *not* been given full disclosure, but during the first few years of subprime escalation, as noted by the account executive, there was little knowledge of or concern about fraud as the market was operating smoothly and the economy appeared healthy. According to over 85% of the interviewees, by the time the market began to expand further during the mid-2000s and competition increased, certain issues (like non-disclosure of loan conditions to borrowers or falsification of income) started to surface that made practitioners question the behavior of their peers and others operating in the business.

Although individual practitioners may have initially possessed a formal yet basic understanding of particular subprime products or services, knowledge on how to manipulate them to their own material advantage followed at later times by less formal means. As one broker alleges:

> A lot of times the reps will come in and explain to you exactly how to submit a loan to make your life easier – to get the loans approved. They're not *encouraging* fraud, nobody *encourages* fraud. But they'll explain to you exactly how to submit it. You know the phrase "I don't want to see the income" because then now if they see the income, they're committing fraud … So that's where a lot of it came into play is "I don't want to see it." It was exactly, "don't ask don't tell."

The respondents agreed that despite this type of "wink, wink" encouragement, their knowledge of fraud, or how people were taking advantage of the subprime in predatory, deceptive, or illegal ways, was not simultaneously diffused with the subprime product knowledge. Consistent with the timeline, over 87% of the interviewees suggested that they did not hear about wholesale fraud in the industry until between the years 2003 and 2005 when ARMs started resetting and default rates began to climb. These default rates increased scrutiny at all levels of the loan transaction and loan securitization process, and many people in the mortgage system became suspicious of what was occurring. As one lender put it, by the mid-2000s "everybody knew what was going on, okay, so it wasn't any secret, everybody knew," whereas others were aware of fraudulent activity well before this time:

> I can tell you that as early as 1991, I had someone come to work for me who had worked in a small shop ... and he had a file that he didn't have all the documentation needed, and at that time came to me and said "where do we keep the blank W-2s?" and I had to say "sit down, let's have a talk" (Originator).

As this originator points out, W-2 and other income misrepresentations, by borrowers, brokers and lenders, has been an ongoing common form of fraud and was not new or unique to the subprime finance industry.

In conclusion, consistent with the respective critical mass points, there was a lag time between first knowledge of subprime products (i.e., the innovation) and first knowledge of a burgeoning subprime fraud problem (i.e., the reinvention).[36] From the interviews it also became evident that subprime fraud was truly a reinvention of the subprime lending innovation rather than an innovation *in and of itself*; specifically, the frauds were made possible through manipulation of the new product and services, and practitioners did not need to develop new opportunities to enable them to use the tools illegally (see discussion in Chapter 9).

Origins of Subprime Diffusion

> **Research Question #4**: *Why and how was the subprime mortgage originally devised and presented to the financial community (e.g., need, source and communication channels) and what is the opportunity structure for this innovation (e.g., who can use it)?*

---

[36] Yet as demonstrated, even when fraud became openly prevalent, subprime lending continued to expand. In fact, 60% of the practitioners noted their disbelief that "nobody did anything about it" when they realized all of the fraud that was going on, but attributed it to the fortunes people were making off the market during that time.

The fourth research question was designed to capture the practitioner's understandings of: (1) how and why subprime lending originated, and how this was presented to them; and, (2) what its opportunity structure was. First, as discussed in Chapter 2, the literature suggests that the notion of subprime mortgage lending may have been originally envisioned during the 1970s and 1980s, yet it did not realistically become a viable lending alternative until the mid-1990s following legislative and regulatory alterations to the Community Reinvestment Act during the Clinton administration. Sixty-seven percent of the interview participants noted this, generally insisting that the idea of extending homeownership to typically unqualified buyers (what they interpreted as an "American Dream" philosophy) was promoted by the government through pressure on banks, lenders, and the GSEs (e.g., Fannie Mae & Freddie Mac) to make more loans to substandard applicants. As one appraiser/lender explains:

> I'll go back to the Clinton era where the policy was "homeownership is an American right. Everyone should be able to own a home. You banks and mortgage companies out there, make it easier for homeownership." And they did. And it was *kids in a candy store* coming up with the mid-prime, the subprime, private mortgage insurance, no money down, low money down – making it *way*, *way* too easy for people to get into houses that never should have been homeowners in the first place.

Another lender agrees, claiming that:

> For the most part, that [subprime lending] originated with the Clinton administration. I remember seeing this in the paper all the time, when the government was screaming "we want programs available to more people who can't get a conventional, fixed-rate loan because they don't have the down payment" … I don't think Fannie Mae just came out and

> said "you know what, we'd like to do 105% loans to people with 600 credit scores," there's no way.

Yet another lender insists that the idea of promoting homeownership was not unique to the Clinton administration, suggesting that *every* president has adhered to this philosophy (in the essence of "political correctness"); the subprime innovation just happened to be formulated and extended during Clinton's reign. However, according to one broker, the accountability for the subprime loan debacle still rests with the Clinton administration:

> Bill Clinton is the one who brought subprime into existence. George Bush catches the flak for it a lot because of the collapse and everything else happened under his watch, but Bill Clinton was the one who actually signed subprime mortgages into law and made them available. And yeah, there was big pressure from the government because the government doesn't want to see an economic downturn. But it still relied on the people, and the business owners, and the big banks to be able to do that. So, you know you work with the tools you are given and the government allowed those tools to come into play, and allowed those people to make millions and millions and millions of dollars, billions of dollars.

The practitioners were unanimous in their contention that subprime lending originated during the mid-1990s when the economy was strong, residential property was plentiful, housing values were reasonable, lending guidelines were relaxed, and government pressure was such that the GSEs were required to open up their portfolios to facilitate lending to individuals who were not traditionally qualified to purchase homes. In combination, this perpetuated the optimistic philosophy and political culture at the time of extending homeownership to basically anyone and everyone who wanted it, and ultimately explains why and how the subprime mortgage was originally presented to the housing industry.

Second, the opportunity structure for subprime lending was not limited to any particular branch of the financial community; if you had the money, you could become a broker or open up a brokerage. As one broker noted:

> To be a loan officer in the state of Wisconsin all you had to have was $250. That's all. There was no education required, there was no criminal background check required, there was nothing. All you needed was $250 and you could be a loan officer. Maybe if you already had a prior felony for fraud or something you wouldn't get accepted, but everybody could be a loan officer. To open up a brokerage you had to have $1,000, basically.

Twenty-seven percent of the respondents noted that up until the early 2000s, smaller, newly formed, non-traditional lending institutions (e.g., subprime specialists) processed the majority of the subprime loans, and the larger banks were not heavily involved. During the mid-90s to the early-2000s, however, a slow and steady entrance of new brokerages was witnessed, as was the expansion of lending alternatives (e.g., low doc/no doc, stated income, Alt-A) by even the more traditional institutions which were also qualified to use the subprime product. As one loan production manager explains:

> It [subprime lending] just kind of came into the common culture around '94/'95 when all of a sudden mortgage brokers really started to come on to the scene. The reason they started taking these loans is because not every, as more and more brokers became licensed as individual brokers, not every one of them could do FHA loans. To do FHA loans you had to open up your books to be audited, so a majority of the brokers out there, if you look at them, I bet you 70% of the brokers did not have the ability to do FHA. So if that's the case (they had) they could potentially do VA, they could do conventional, but they were missing FHA, so they had to find another "gun in their arsenal" to work with, so that's why they started getting involved.

According to the respondents, aside from corporate constraints, there were really no legal limitations as to who could utilize the subprime lending tools. They were very popular as they presented product and service opportunities for individuals and businesses that could not otherwise provide these under traditional mortgage lending practices (e.g., FHA). In sum, one account executive puts this entire opportunity structure into perspective: "If you've got someone who's willing to supply you with a product and buy it from you, and you've got willing customers, most businessmen would take that opportunity in a second."

In conclusion, according to the respondents, the subprime mortgage was originally devised to facilitate and increase homeownership to a segment of the population that had historically not been capable of achieving this element of the "American Dream." Through articulation of governmental philosophy, as manifested in and communicated through legislation and relaxed regulation and lending standards, as well as through the growth in the number of willing buyers and subsidized avenues for passing on risk (e.g., through Fannie Mae & Freddie Mac), the subprime innovation was presented to the financial community as a need for the American economy and its people. Thus, the opportunity structure presented by subprime lending alternatives not only extended to new and existing real estate and mortgage-related enterprises, but to the U.S. citizenry as well.

Subprime Characteristics

> **Research Question #5**: *What characteristics of the subprime lending innovation contributed to its rate and extent of adoption, and what characteristics contributed to fraud in the market due to its diffusion and its reinvention?*

Question five encompasses two separate issues that were presented to the interview participants. The first issue is concerned with identifying the attributes of subprime lending which influenced individuals and companies to begin using it, while the second issue seeks to identify the characteristics that may have enabled these parties to manipulate it. These are discussed individually below.

As demonstrated above, the growth in subprime lending was slow throughout the 1990s. As the literature reveals, at the turn of the century and continuing on through the events of 9/11, however, the economy became unstable and the financial and housing markets wavered. To facilitate confidence and renewed energy within these markets, interest rates were lowered, and, as noted by over one-quarter of the interviewees, borrowing and home ownership were further encouraged, this time by the Bush administration. Sixty-seven percent of the interview respondents explained that as demand for mortgage-backed securities also began to rise (e.g., willing buyers), and the success of the securities sales to global markets became realized, a new wave of brokerages, as well as prime, or traditionally conservative, lenders entered the subprime market. Within a short period of time, the critical mass of adopters had been reached, and the volume of subprime originations and other higher-risk alternatives skyrocketed.

One lender explains that following the refinancing craze of the 1990s, to take advantage of these newer alternative and lower-than-prime lending opportunities and to stimulate more business, lenders began to creatively seek out new customers and products; subprime lending enabled this resourcefulness. This also helps to explain the varying levels of annual subprime refinances versus purchase originations as highlighted above.

> The industry ran through the prime borrowers and then everyone refinanced that could refinance. And lenders sat back and said "there's other pretty good qualified borrowers out there, maybe they missed a payment here or there, their credit scores aren't at that average, that 680 average, they've got scores between say 650 and 680, we'll call them *mid-prime*. And because they've had some blemishes, we'll still do mortgages for them, but we'll charge a little bit higher rate to mitigate our potential losses."
>
> So mid-prime lending was done for those individuals that had a few blemishes on their credit report. Rates still remained low. The majority of those types of borrowers were run

> through; more handwringing, "we have to make more money, so let's do *subprime* lending. Credit scores in the 600 to 650 range, and again they've had problems, more problems than the mid-prime borrowers, but they deserve a mortgage, so we'll charge a little bit more interest rate, maybe do adjustable rate mortgages, different types of lending programs to get them into houses, and again to try to reduce our risk, we'll charge higher rates" (Loan Officer/Former Appraiser).

Consistent with this respondent's conclusions, the profitability of subprime lending (through higher fees and interest rates) was credited by 73% of the interviewees as the number one factor which eventually motivated the adoption of the tool by all facets of the industry. Examples of the profitability at the individual transaction level were provided by most of the interviewees, such as the increased points an originator or broker could make on a subprime (e.g., 8%) versus the income on a traditional loan closing (e.g., 3%). The profitability from the corporate perspective was also explained, especially on loans that exceeded the value of the property (i.e., over 100% loan-to-value ratio):

> [A]n appraisal class I was sitting in, and it had to have been in 2003, or 2001 ... the instructor said at that time "do you appraisers understand why these lenders are doing 100% loans?" Traditionally again it was an 80%, you've got to have 20% down. "100, 105, 110, 120% LTVs?" And everyone raised their hand and said "no, what is going on?" "Well, let's look at 100 million in loans at an 80% loan-to-value. Now do that same block of loans at 120% of value. If you can gain 40% more like that, in an era when foreclosure rates are *infinitesimal*, what's the risk? Why not go to that 100, 120%?" Because again, at the time, it was just go, go, go (Loan Officer/Former Appraiser).

The ability to pass the subprime loan risk to the secondary market in this scenario, and as noted by the account executive above (i.e., when there is someone willing to buy a product from you), was also credited by respondents as a major factor in the willingness of companies to partake in higher-risk lending. But even on a more basic level, as concerns over stability and profitability were heightened, mortgage industry professionals began to fear (and experience) the loss of business to the "guy down the street," and competition escalated. As one bank sales manager pointed out though, "if you are working somewhere where you have a competitive rate, you do not have to be the best, just be competitive and do a good job."

When the bigger lenders experienced a loss of revenues to the subprime market, and witnessed the financial rewards to the subprime lenders through the early 2000s, many of them got on board and began developing their own versions of subprime and other alternative loan products. As one broker contends:

> [T]here was a point in time maybe, seven years ago, FHA was worried that it wouldn't be sustainable, because so many of these brokers were taking business that should have, could have, would have, gone FHA that went subprime, that FHA was wondering how they were going to be able to do enough business to sustain itself. So they started to relax the rules, and Fannie Mae and Freddie Mac? They were concerned as well. So, what did they do? They started doing what were called Alt-A loans and they relaxed *their* rules.

Yet there is evidence of a more involved explanation, similar to what the broker pointed out above, which helps to illuminate the growing political pressure on the financial industry that encouraged some of these companies to partake in the expanding subprime market in the early 2000s:

> It [U.S. government] needed to compete because Fannie Mae and Freddie Mac are corporations. They are publicly-traded companies which means they have to make money somehow, right? So they needed to make money … how can you make more money? They were losing more and more business, so was FHA, losing more and more business to subprime. And

> you know the brokers, they sure as heck didn't want to get into FHA, they didn't need it! They were doing all these loans, they were getting all these investors here working outside the norm, and they're selling all these loans, to God knows where, and everybody's making money (Lender).

In addition to profitability, other characteristics of subprime lending that contributed to its rate and extent of adoption was that the alternative loan products (e.g., pay-option ARMs, Alt-A loans, "Fast & Easy") were compatible and not difficult to implement or use,[37] and could rather easily be incorporated into a business entity's existing lending *repertoire*. Besides the straight subprime companies who may or may not have been FHA approved, other lenders could actually experiment with the subprime market with little capital infusion or organizational restructuring. As 40% of the respondents pointed out, for many years, every institution had at least one "guy" who specialized in alternative loans, while other companies expanded operations as demand and commitment to the subprime market rose.

But not all lenders jumped on board or relaxed their rules to adopt subprime lending, especially the locally owned or community banks, as pointed out by more than half of the interviewees. For example, "the smaller institutions would take less risk, they knew what their niche was, and you stick with your niche and you move on. As a larger company, you know, again, stockholders are a big part of that; income is a big part of that; more profits, more money" (Lender). Other interviewees agreed, with one broker noting:

> They [local banks] won't take that kind of risk because they've got auto loans, they have credit cards, they have toy loans, like motorcycles and boats and four-wheelers. They've

[37] As one lender explains: "We had people coming into the mortgage industry that never had an idea of how to lend. You know mortgage lending, it really comes down to a pretty simple concept, there is simply a checklist and if things go into that checklist, you get them done, and that's mortgage lending. Simple ratios and things like that."

> got money coming in from all different avenues, so they don't need to; the private lending institutions I don't think ever fell down to this subprime level because there is just no need for them to take any kind of risk like that.

Two others concurred, also suggesting that local/community banks (and by extension, their employees) resisted the opportunity to adopt subprime lending due to their existing organizational structures and priorities.

In sum, the interviewees agreed that competition, profit margin concerns, ease of use, and compatibility contributed to the speed at which even traditional lenders entered the subprime market and the cut-throat climate it produced. For example, one lender explains how competition, profitability goals, and fiscal health interact to influence corporate behavior:

> … when you see another institution shows their fourth-quarter earnings were double yours and you're the same size … "well, what are we not doing? … they're in the subprime market … we need to get into the subprime market."

Eighty-seven percent of the respondents also noted that subprime attributes influenced not only the financial community to adopt, but they also influenced borrowers. With the subprime and alternative loans now available, "a huge demographic of people that now qualified for loans" (Broker) entered the picture and wanted in on the potential benefits the subprime provided. One respondent points out:

> Property values were continuing to rise. People were able to access the equity in their home rather easily, and they had uncontrollable spending debt. So they said "okay I can knock off all of this, and save up to $1,000 a month" whatever it was, while paying off all this credit card debt, making a tax deduction now because it's mortgage interest, and it just made

> sense and they just kept racking it up and racking it up (Account Executive).

These types of lender and borrower attitudes about subprime's profitability, ease of use, and increased competition were also seen from the real estate market side as well. For example,

> I mean the lenders were just … out of their minds making all these loans … I can remember walking around the office here, and there was one agent, and he was kind of a comical kind of guy, and he used to say "there's *free* money out there, everybody's got *free* money, you know you don't have to do *anything* for it." I mean literally we reached a time where it was easier to get a loan on a home than it was to get a car loan. I mean that is just *unheard* of (Realtor).

As such, the potential advantages of subprime lending became evident to not only industry practitioners, but also to governmental entities, policymakers, and current and potential home buyers. But just as these perceived benefits of subprime lending contributed to its rate and extent of adoption, they may also have inadvertently facilitated fraud within the industry for some of the very same reasons as the lending practice spread throughout the country.

Part two of the fifth research question examines the characteristics and availability of subprime lending and how these may have contributed to the amount or types of fraud that have been linked to it. As subprime lending became available to a greater variety of practitioners and borrowers throughout the early 2000s, many of these industry insiders and customers eventually found ways to take "advantage of the opportunities that were put in front of them" (Lender). Although profitability and greed may have contributed to the rate and extent of adoption of subprime lending, greed itself was cited by 60% of the respondents as the number one reason people manipulated the process (fraudulent or predatory) for their own gain (profit or property). Some pointed out the breadth of this greed, for example:

> ... cut and dried, greed, from many different levels. From the banks lending the loans to sell on the secondary market, to the profitability and the point spread on the loans, to the broker needing to up-sale the rate or the margins on these loans to get more points, to the borrower trying to get the best possible scenario to qualify for (Account Executive).

As this executive suggests, this quest for unprecedented monetary and material wealth permeated throughout the mortgage and financial communities, as well as throughout the population of existing, new, and potential homeowners. Yet the perceived lack of risk and ease at which fraud could be committed by any number of these involved parties also contributed to *its* rate and extent as the innovation traversed the mortgage lending system. What requires more explanation is how the characteristics of subprime lending facilitated deception by enabling individuals or groups to take advantage of the opportunity, and what factors contributed to their motivation or willingness to do so.

The interview participants approached this topic from a variety of perspectives. Besides noting greed, 67% argued that the lack of regulation enforcement and the low probability of being caught contributed to the amount of fraud that accompanied the subprime mortgage process. Many explained that due to the overwhelming volume of loan processing occurring during the expansion of the subprime market, oversight and accountability were negligible. For example, one originator claims that:

> ... because of relaxation and guidelines, and the demand upon Fannie and Freddie to take looser approaches, lenders came to me and said "we'll allow you to approve loans in your office, without having to send them to us." I chose not to do that; I didn't want the liability that came with it, and they have people that are better trained in that area than I am to underwrite those files, determine applicable guidelines.

As noted above, there were also too many new players and transactions to keep track of, and fraudulent deals could be easily passed on with little threat of detection, or even if detected with little threat of serious consequences. In reality, for many the clear benefits from fraud tended to exceed the limited risks. One account executive provides a good example of this:

> We had groups of brokers we watched … groups of people that tended to work together that would, they would work under one name, like ABC mortgage or whatever, just throwing out random names, in a certain location for say one to two years until it got pretty well known that nothing but fraud was coming out of there, then they would shut down, move to another little city, maybe 20 minutes away, change their name, start up all over again. So there really wasn't very much, I mean there is always the potential risk of the Feds coming in for whatever reason, but there was very little oversight.

Granted, it is probably safe to assume that the majority of practitioners and borrowers did not engage in fraud during their involvement with subprime or other related mortgage products. As one out of three interviewees noted, ethics and a sense of morality, or the willingness to not put your own job at risk, undoubtedly deterred the majority of industry practitioners from ever knowingly participating in fraudulent transactions. One broker also pointed out that business was so good for a time that you did not need to be greedy or commit fraud to experience gain, even from the borrower's perspective:

> As far as fraud goes, there wasn't a need for a lot of fraud. What fraud do you need if you have a 580 credit score and a bank's saying "yeah, we'll get you a 100% purchase as long as you have three open trade lines and a 580 credit score." At that time in the economy, you'd almost have to purposely destroy yourself to not qualify. So the qualifications were there, so there was really no need for fraud, there just wasn't. There was no need for fraud because … if 50 people came to

> me in a month, and half of them qualified (and half of them did), there's no need, it's not like I'm starving for business. At $3,000 a deal, with 25 of them closing, ... that's plenty of money for me, so why would I need to risk my license and my livelihood and the way that I feed my family by producing a W-2 that's fraudulent? I wouldn't need to do that, I would just tell that person "you don't qualify" and move onto the next call, or the next 10 people that I haven't had time to qualify yet.

Another originator agrees, indicating that working legitimately he paid more in taxes in 2003 than he *made* in total income in many adjacent years. But as established, countless individuals *did* participate in illegal activity because, as pointed out by the interviewees, subprime misrepresentations (e.g., falsifying records that they knew would not be verified) provided the opportunity to feed the greed, and there was a perceived low risk of fraud ever being detected.

Moreover, fraud was not only easy to commit, it was enabled by many of the very characteristics of the subprime products themselves. Requirements for the subprime loan transaction as well as other mortgage products (e.g., Alt-A; Countrywide's "Fast & Easy"), had been reduced to the point that little or no documentation was needed in many cases. As one banker describes it, "It was so easy. I would always like to say that if you had a pulse, you could get a loan." For example, many of the practitioners suggested that the stated income loan, originally designed for the self-employed borrower, was eventually used predatorily for almost any W-2 borrower (those who could provide full income documentation and qualify for better terms). Although fraud was not encouraged with this type of loan expectation, where the borrower and originator *could* put down virtually any figure that they thought would be accepted by underwriters, and there were avenues (e.g., salary.com) for validating the viability of the income estimate, this type of validation to prevent deception was not required or occurring.

Furthermore, motivated originators could use their normal organizational routines to put forth false statements and make a subprime transaction appear legitimate with little fear of detection due to the unprecedented volume of applications that were going through the loan and securitization process during the time (Originator). As one lender argues, "if it could have all the pretenses of being a legitimate loan, from the appraisal, to the title, to the real estate agent and such, and those things were [able to be] sold in the marketplace." One lender and an originator also indicated that computer technology enabled motivated home buyers and brokers to produce false and deceptive documents (e.g., artificial bank statements or W-2s) much more easily and readily than when all real estate transaction documentation was done by hand.

Yet it was not even a lack attention to verification that was problematic, as interviewees noted. It was the lack of the *requirement* for verification. For example, one lender noted that underwriters were not required in many instances to verify, and an originator suggests that this extended into traditional mortgage products for a time as well:

> The "Fast & Easy" program that we did, that was a conforming loan, it was just a regular conventional, but it was all stated, there was no verification done. We verify they worked, but we didn't verify how much they made, we did not verify assets – it was just all stated income, stated assets. And then you had other programs, they were called no income, no asset loans, and stated income, stated asset loans. No income, no assets ... that's what it was, you filled out an application, you didn't put income down, you didn't put assets down, it was all left blank, and that's how you closed them.

So, as surmised by 93.3% of the respondents, based on their respective experiences, the ability of the borrowers and originators (be they brokers or bankers) to *state* income rather than provide evidence of the borrower's income (or assets, or liabilities, or intentions, etc.) and the ability of the underwriters to approve these notes without verification contributed to a substantial portion of the temptation to commit, and the actual committed fraud, in the U.S. mortgage industry. This repeated conclusion of the interviewees is compatible with FinCEN's findings that over 50% of the reported frauds committed even after the subprime demise (between 2007 and 2009) have been due to the combination of income, asset, and liability misrepresentations (see Table 7.1). One can understand that if there is that much fraud occurring with the more recent and stringent full documentation requirements, the extent of fraud during subprime's heyday was possibly even more substantial than what continues to be estimated.

And finally, in addition to the ease at with which fraud could be committed under the guise of low- and no-documentation lending, subprime characteristics attracted a certain type of borrower that may have been more easily swindled than traditional mortgage customers. As one broker alleges:

> Subprime made it easier to commit those types of fraud because subprime allowed a lesser clientele into the picture … well-educated, financially responsible people are harder to trick than lower income people. And again, I'm at the risk here of sounding very discriminatory, but I'm not, it's plain and simple ... so yeah you're talking, your blue collar, your less educated, your lower income people that now, even if you read the contracts word-for-word they might not even understand it. They're not going to say "I don't understand this," they're not going to go get, they don't even have money to put down on the house, they're not going to go out and hire an attorney. So I think it's just less educated.

Two other lenders also stated that undereducated, naïve, or desperate borrowers made it easier for practitioners to trick them, and for things to be passed by them without detection, even when others in the industry knew or suspected fraud was being committed:

> You know some of the customers came in and questioned some of the fees from some of these people, and some of them walked away, and a lot of them signed because they felt they

> had to. Most borrowers don't read any documentation; a lot of them don't understand it. A lot of them figure if they are walking into a lender, whether it's an independent broker or part of a bank, they simply trust. ... I've been lending for 30 years and I've only had two or three people who ever actually read the documents ... Simply sign, and sometimes they don't have a choice: "You want to buy the house or not? It's closing today, these are the documents, you sign them or else it doesn't get done." So they were strong-armed sometimes into accepting what was presented to them ... at that point, you know they probably, they might've even have sold their other house, and didn't have a choice (Lender).

In sum, the characteristics of the subprime innovation (e.g., ease of use, low oversight), and the ability of practitioners to manipulate it by using deception to take advantage of borrowers' naivety and oftentimes own fraudulent pursuit of material gain, further demonstrates the flexibility of the tool to be easily utilized in unintended ways. The interviewees generally agreed that profitability and greed, the ability to pass the subprime loan risk to the secondary market, and the ease with which subprime lending could be integrated into the existing mortgage industry and related institutional operations are the principal characteristics that combine to explain the rate and extent of the adoption of subprime lending. Similarly, greed, or getting more than you needed, as fulfilled through the profitability of subprime in general, and more specifically to its fraudulent application, as well as the low risk of detection of, and punishment for, fraud and the ease at which it could be committed, all combine to help explain the fraud that has accompanied it.

Communication Channels

> **Research Question #6**: *What communication channels (e.g., formal or informal) have been most likely to diffuse the legitimate as compared to the illegitimate applications of the innovation?*

As discussed in Questions #3 and #4 above subprime lending was presented to mortgage and real estate practitioners and the public by official industry channels, such as cold-calls, training seminars, and media outlets. It should be noted that these communicated messages were not necessarily entitled "subprime" as it is now understood, but would rather outline specific attributes of the products, such as no money down, or no income verification needed, and would basically give the impression that there were loans out there to fulfill the needs of just about any type of interested originator or buyer.

In order to address the sixth research question, the interviewees were asked to share how they learned of the tools and applications of subprime lending through various communication channels. Communication is defined here as the process of information-sharing and the channels are the means by which this communication occurs, ranging from formal (e.g., industry publications, advertising, and official training and sales contacts), to informal (e.g., one-on-one conversations, and grapevine or word-of-mouth information). Interviewees explained these channels in various ways. For example, subprime lender account representatives were a popular communication source:

> The lenders would have what we call account executives, mortgage reps, that would come to the office, explain why we should use them, what programs they offered, that maybe somebody else didn't offer, and everybody had the bulk of the same, you know 80% of the loans were the same, but every company had their own couple niches. Maybe this one, Company A, would go down to a 500 credit score, where Company B might only go down to 550 or 560 at the time. This company might do 100%, stated income, where this company would only do 80%, but they would do something else. So they all had their own couple of niche programs which kept them as a necessity in the market (Broker).

> The companies, they did not necessarily have conferences, but all of the lenders, whether they be A-Paper lenders, subprime lenders, or Alt-A lenders, they all had account reps, who would come in and … would say "here's what we will accept – we will accept a stated income loan, with a 580 credit score as long as they have been employed at their job for the last two years or self-employed as long as the state will acknowledge that their company has been around for two years." So that's how they'd learn it; they were basically being taught it by the investors, by the sales people who were coming and saying we can do just about any loan that there is out there (Lender).

> They [account executives] would come in, let's say whatever it is, Countrywide, Bank of America, all of the ones that are around, and Wells [Fargo], and they'd come in. And all the BC lenders would come in, they, a lot of times, they'd hold seminars … I don't remember the guy's name, but he came into town and he had maybe 200 people in the room and he was giving all his guidelines for his company and what loans they would make. So that's how we got a lot of it, is a new company would come in and do this, or, you'd have a company where, for example, right now, one that's around that still, is, you know, [XXX], a local bank. They send a rep over to the company and they say "hey, we've got this new program." They'll do maybe a one-hour class on some Thursday or whatever, bring lunch, and that's what we do. So there were a lot of luncheons where they'd come and talk about their programs (Broker).

These types of experiences were reported by 60% of the respondents, who also noted that many alternative financing structures came to their attention through "rate sheets" that were personally distributed or made available via the Internet.[38]

In contrast to the more formal communications of the legitimate applications of subprime lending, and the original acquisition of knowledge about the subprime and its reinvention (see Question #3), informal communications alone were noted by over 73% of the interviewees as the means in which they learned the actual "in-and-outs" of how they could partake in illegitimate applications of the tools if they so desired. Most of this communication occurred during the socialization and training process, while a lot also occurred during the individual's day-to-day interactions with people in the mortgage business (occupational, organizational, and/or industry contacts). Below are some examples of this communication process as shared by the interviewees:

> We did not have an employee meeting from the corporation, or company telling us what to do and how to do it … the ones that were honest knew it, could see the other ones doing that, you could tell. And some of them would actually tell you what they're doing, so I mean there was word-of-mouth of what was going on (Lender).

> Every company … had a guy. "You need bank statements, go to this guy … you need $10,000 more on an appraisal, use this guy." So then new people came in to the industry and they saw this behavior going on so they aped it because those people were top producers and making a lot of money (Account Executive).

> … we heard stories, because people change jobs a lot and would tell us what was going on in their back office at other

---

[38] Visit www.53.com for an example of a recent (publicly available) rate sheet from Fifth Third Bank (Fifth Third Bank, 2010).

> places … I would say it [the type of communication] is more subtle than that though, more of a sort of an understanding … It's more of a wink-and-nod kind of thing like "I'll take care of you, start sending me your business and I'll make sure …" And it doesn't take you more than a couple of months to figure out, and you have friends in the business usually who can tell you "hey, we got this new guy from Company C, they'll take care of you, start sending them business" and all of a sudden you would just see massive shifts, all of the business going, boom, there (Account Executive).

> I think it starts with relationships. You build relationships … if a realtor is in with a builder, and when building was great, and being a realtor was great, it was bread-and-butter, the realtor passes the name of a lender, the lender and the builder all know each other, and there [were] some things going on behind the scenes that I think, that's what kept this going (Lender).

But sometimes the way to "massage" a loan, whether legitimately or illegitimately was informally communicated directly by the account executives, and/or originators learned by trial and error:

> … your reps will tell you. A perfect example, I'm a young loan officer and I'm just kind of learning the business and I have a client and they qualify and I have all their income documentation and everything else, and your rep comes in and you go "okay, I have all this, "well, we don't need that, we'll just do it stated, there is no difference. If you send me these W-2s or whatever, we're going to have to order VOE's [Verification of Employment], we're going to need updated pay stubs, we are going to need all this extra stuff and it's going to make no difference on the loan. So just leave it out, send it in stated, it'll be the exact same loan, except for you don't have to do all this extra work."
> Well you accidentally send that stuff in, and they find something on it that you didn't even know about, and now

> your deal is dead, at *that* lender. Now you just learned to not send it into the next lender, and now it's approved. But that's because one particular underwriter looked at something different and didn't want to do it. So maybe they [buyer] were only on their job for a year and 11 months, and they're working 20 hours of overtime every week, but the rule is you have to be on your job for two years in order to include overtime income. So that gets thrown out, now your debt to asset ratio doesn't work, but you can do it stated, but that lender won't do it because now they've seen the income (Broker).

In sum, formal and informal communications channels were the most likely to diffuse the legitimate applications of subprime lending, whereas informal channels (e.g., unofficial versions of how to use or manipulate the products, network associations) were the most likely avenues for communicating the illegitimate applications of subprime lending.

Reinvention of Subprime

> **Research Question** #7: *Are there characteristics of subprime lending which make it more likely to be re-invented for fraudulent purposes than other mortgage tools and techniques (e.g., prime loans)?*

The seventh research question is quite similar to the second component of question five on subprime attributes, but this question taps into the practitioners' understandings of the differences between the characteristics and opportunities provided by subprime that are not found in traditional lending practices or products. As outlined in the discussion of Question #5 above, from borrowers on up, the ability of participants in the mortgage process to commit fraud was facilitated by the characteristics of both the subprime products and process, as well as by characteristics of individuals involved in the transactions.

Over two-thirds of the respondents noted that although there has always been fraud in the industry you could not necessarily commit the types and levels of fraud with traditional loans (which required full disclosure and documentation) that you could with subprime. With the subprime no documentation/no verification stated income type loans, "the system set itself up for itself to be taken advantage of, and nobody cared, as long as property values were going up, and there was an acceptable level of foreclosures" (Lender). There were also other aspects of the market that developed during this time which some believe contributed to the record amounts of fraudulent misrepresentations:

> There is always a criminal element, the white collar element, there is [a] white collar criminal element at every different level, but mortgage sales people became the aluminum siding sales people from the '70s – that same person kind of gravitated into this. Okay, because there were no licensing requirements, there were no background checks, there was none of that stuff, so you could have somebody who couldn't be a bank teller, but was obtaining Social Security ID numbers.
>
> So the opportunity for people, there is just a certain element of people that are going to just go "I've got the opportunity, I am going to take advantage of it" … that element is just out there … it was never policed in the beginning. Because nobody could believe that … it got to the point where, I view my house first and foremost as shelter. Not an investment, not a way to get me out of trouble financially, it is shelter, without it, you're homeless. That got lost somewhere along the line from the borrower's standpoint, "how do I get out of trouble, my buddy Bob over here just told me he refinanced his house with [XXX] Mortgage, and his interest rate might be higher, but oh my God, he got all of his other problems gone; he was able to pay off his car, he was even able to skip two months of house payments … wow, how much better would that be" (Lender)?

As this lender suggests, in addition to the actual characteristics of subprime that made it more likely to be reinvented for fraudulent gain than more regulated and traditional lending, there was also a pervasive attitude and climate which developed in the industry *and* in society which perpetuated unethical, predatory, and fraudulent behavior. Again, this was not only based on profitability and competition, but on greed. The interview participants were unanimous in their belief that this attitude or greed mindset contributed to: (1) the willingness of individuals to reinvent the subprime process for illegitimate gain; (2) the extent of fraud witnessed in the subprime industry; and, (3) to the speed at which it permeated the U.S. culture.

Regulation

> **Research Question #8**: *What types of regulatory controls could have been included in the original innovation or its diffusion (innovation-decision) process to minimize the risk of its use for illegal gains?*

This eighth and final research question posed a challenge to many participants, as many believe that subprime facilitated *predatory* behavior, not just fraud, and they find it is difficult for most people to disentangle the two. For example, when asked about how the initial loosening of regulations (e.g., credit requirements; broker licensing) may have "made it easier to manipulate or easier to take advantage of these loans?" one broker argued:

> What made it easier? When they got to the point of where a lender would say "we don't have to verify the income, we don't have to verify the assets, we don't have to verify anything; basically they have a name and Social Security number, we'll take their word for it." But, in the true sense of the word, there was no *fraud* committed – because the lender said "don't tell us how much they make, don't tell us anything, we'll just give you the loan." They [originators] were making

> loans *exactly* how the lenders wanted them to make loans and the borrowers were getting money *exactly* how the lenders wanted them to get money.

As noted above, others agree with this depiction of the subprime and its application over time; besides the ability of just about anyone to enter into transactions, it was not necessarily a lack of regulation that created opportunities for fraud, but rather the structure of the subprime products and process itself that contributed to the risk of it being used illicitly. As others noted:

> They wanted you to make loans to all different types of people and I think that turned into "you need to make loans to *everybody*." And the reality is – you don't. You need to make loans to people that number one, deserve it, and show a history that they can do that, and if they don't, you don't make that loan (Lender).

> I think essentially what we had was a situation where, for example Fannie Mae and Freddie Mac, lowered the requirements to get a loan – low credit scores, no down payment, things like that. They put a combination of things together and allowed a loan to go forward for somebody [that] that most people with common sense would know that these people were not going to be able to make these payments. So the requirements were just loosened just to an impractical point. I think the business operates, has operated for many, many years, 30-40 years, based on certain requirements, you know having a certain level of credit, your income qualifying you for a payment at certain levels, and usually that involves something like 30-40% total debt ratios as compared to what you earn per month. So I mean we had loans going out to people that had debts that were, they had total debts that were in the 50s, I mean it was *bound* to be a problem (Realtor).

Besides the regulatory inattention to risk, this realtor also suggested the lack of required transparency in the system (e.g., not fully disclosing loan conditions to borrowers; underestimating the risk in bundled loans during securitization) was problematic:

> [I]t was unbelievable. And you know the other bad sign for us that we knew we were going to run into a problem (because we could see this coming), and what surprised us is that there wasn't anybody doing anything about trying to stop it.

The loan and real estate closing process itself was also confusing and overwhelming to borrowers, and the details of the transactions were not readily apparent to many buyers, like full disclosure on potential prepayment penalties:

> People sign so many papers at a closing that this prepayment rider meant nothing to them, and then they would be so huge that they couldn't finance it – they didn't have the equity to do it at that point (Bank Sales Manager).

Less than one-third of the respondents argued that regulation could have been increased, specifically on the non-depository banking (brokerage) side of things, but *all* of the interviewees agreed that existing regulation could have been *enforced* throughout the entire mortgage process (including rating and securitization) in a more timely manner than what was witnessed to curb some of the fraudulent and substandard lending practices:

> I work in a banking institution so that's the benefit I have, we have regulations, we get regulated more than anybody else out there, so from a broker side of it we didn't have to go through some of the audits and some things that *now* they're going through, we've always been going through that process (Lender).

> I don't know if at the broker shops, you had your own underwriters maybe, but in banks, you've got an underwriting

> *staff.* Did it [fraud] happen? I'm sure it happened. Was there a lot of pressure on people to do loans? Yes. But no one wanted a loan to be done in the banking industry with fraud because you don't know when a file is going to be pulled for an audit behind the scene, and they *will* verify what that person makes, and they *will* pull their tax returns (Bank Sales Manager).

As one lender pointed out, the attention to regulation and the product structure came "a little too late" in both the banks and brokerages, and ultimately came from external pressure. The lender noted that "the investors started seeing delinquency rates rise on mortgages and they started to throw in their own safeguards, but it was not until they had to."

In sum, the respondents generally agreed that the willingness of the financial and mortgage industries, investors, and home buyers to accept the subprime mortgage product, and all of the monetary risk that was associated with it, was the major contributor to the fraud which accompanied it, rather than the lack of established regulation. As evidenced by the tightening of existing regulation, and increased surveillance and enforcement, perceptions about fraud risk may be changing:

> Risk/reward has definitely changed, especially over the last year. You know some of the prosecutions that have gone on, that have people that flat-out committed fraud and admitted it and it's proven, you know you're in jail three to five years. All of a sudden a slap on the wrist, or a $100,000 fine, when you made $3 or $4 million over that period of time – write the check and move on – now you're going to jail, it's a big difference … I believe it is, but you're still going to have a few shysters that are going to try and move in, but I think, and again when you're dealing with a local individual, a local institution, "I live in your neighborhood, I'm not going to set you up to fail" (Lender).

The enforcement of the regulations that have been on the books, as well as civil and criminal law, is demonstrating that amplifying the pressure on the industry to correct itself may have been beneficial to a certain degree during the time of escalating fraud, at least in terms of an individual's risk/benefit calculations.

CHAPTER 9

Attributes of Subprime Lending and Fraud

One of the primary objectives of the current study was to examine the process through which subprime lending and subprime fraud developed and spread throughout the mortgage industry, and how the factors associated with this process coalesced to form a "house of cards" that ended in the meltdown of the subprime mortgage industry (see CBS, 2008). Descriptive public-access data and practitioner interviews were utilized to accomplish this goal, and similar to the strategy employed by Baker and Faulkner (2003) in their investigation of intermediate fraud in a gas and oil business, diffusion theory was used to guide the examination of the rate and extent of subprime mortgage lending and its associated fraud in the U.S. over the past twenty years.

As discussed previously, diffusion of innovations theory (Rogers, 2003) outlines a variety of factors which are consistently found to be correlated with the spread of new ideas through social systems. These include a host of variables in a five-stage innovation-decision process, variables associated with the perceived attributes of an innovation, and those determining the rate of innovation adoption (see Figures 4.1 and 4.2).

In contrast to Baker and Faulkner (2003), however, criminological theory was also utilized here to structure the data collection and analysis, most notably with respect to various opportunity, associations, and routines factors found in Differential Association (Sutherland, 1983), Routine Activities (Cohen & Felson, 1979), Rational Choice (Clarke & Cornish, 1985), and Social Learning (Akers, 1990) theories. Aspects of situational crime prevention (Clarke, 1980; Benson, Madensen, & Eck, 2009) and the white collar crime opportunity perspective (e.g., techniques and properties; see Benson & Simpson, 2009) were also considered and helped guide the study. These criminological concepts are incorporated into the ensuing discussion which will interpret the study results from the diffusion perspective.

The discussion is organized around the innovation characteristics of relative advantage, compatibility, complexity, trialability, and observability, which in combination help to explain both the decision to adopt the subprime innovation and subprime fraud, and account for the rate of their respective diffusions across the mortgage system. These five variables were selected as they have been shown to contribute to more explained adoption variance than all other diffusion model variables combined (Rogers, 2003), and they capture the essence of the subprime lending process and its fraudulent reinvention as articulated by the study participants.

Relative Advantage

Relative advantage is defined in diffusion theory as "the degree to which an innovation is perceived as being better than the idea that supersedes it" (Rogers, 2003:15). It was demonstrated throughout the interviews with mortgage practitioners that the subprime mortgage innovation provided perceived improvements over traditional lending in that it: (1) increased economic profitability; (2) provided an avenue by which historically unqualified parties could qualify for home loans; (3) opened up new employment opportunities for mortgage and real estate practitioners; and, (4) enabled the creation of numerous alternative loan structures that were convenient and relatively easy to use.

First, subprime lending increased economic profitability. The innovation created opportunities for every facet of the mortgage food chain (Bitner, 2008) to benefit financially in terms of property or profit. In contrast to traditional loans, home buyers could now obtain property with little to no money down, home owners could use the equity in their property to cash-out and pay off higher interest debt, to purchase other desirable assets (e.g., car, boats), or to use the funds in any way they saw fit (e.g., vacations). Conventional and non-depository lenders could offer a wider variety of loan structure options, while allowing them to pass on the risk associated with these products out of their own portfolios and into the secondary market. In turn, they would benefit from the origination premiums and servicing fees of the subprime notes. And finally, the secondary market, including the investors, GSEs, rating agencies, financial institutions, and investment managers (e.g., hedge or pension funds) were provided with increased revenue alternatives that many perceived as having unlimited potential. This profitability finding is consistent with the previously cited findings of Mansfield (1961) and Diamond (2003).

Granted, the concept or "risk" as used above, has different meanings when discussing the innovation (risk of financial loss – decreased profitability) as compared to its reinvention (risk of detection and punishment), yet it could be argued that the risk represents a relative *disadvantage* in either situation. However, the reinvention of subprime lending through fraud (e.g., fake W-2s, misrepresentation of assets, occupancy, etc.) also provided perceived relative advantages over traditional lending schemes in terms of increased economic profitability, with little risk of detection or punishment. As noted by the interviewees, from the borrowers on up, individuals could more readily partake in fraudulent applications for subprime mortgages to improve their material and/or monetary positions. In sum, the respondents argued that the advantages presented with the subprime and its illegitimate uses could fulfill the greed that appeared to overtake the housing industry, the financial markets, and the citizenry in the early 2000s, with little perceived disadvantage.

Second, subprime lending was relatively advantageous as compared to traditional lending as it provided an avenue by which historically unqualified buyers could now qualify for home loans. In fact, the government was consistently noted by the interviewees as promoting this American Dream philosophy through its regulatory and legislative activity, as well as through its insistence that the GSEs and banks make these less-restrictive lending options available. This created new opportunities for individuals who would not have normally been involved in mortgage transactions to benefit from their existence in terms of homeownership, and also increased opportunities for homeowners to take advantage of the refinance and cash-out options with fraudulent loan applications through the low/no document, stated income type products.

Third, a perceived relative advantage of the subprime market was that it opened up new and increased employment opportunities for mortgage and real estate practitioners. As one lender commented, "the subprime and all the mortgage brokers and all that came about when the savings and loan collapsed. That's when brokers started. You know how many brokers there were in like 1985? Like two. Seriously." As noted in the results, other respondents also commented on the entrance of untold numbers of new brokers, brokerages, loan officers, subprime specialty companies, and the like as the subprime innovation began its ascent through the U.S. markets in the 1990s. The secondary advantage of this aspect of subprime lending was that it allowed companies to increase their sales forces, especially with eager commissioned staff. These factors also contributed to the perceived benefits of participation by these parties in the reinvention of the subprime innovation, in terms of their ability to take advantage of the lower levels of regulation and guardianship within the industry due to the rapid expansion of the industry and the sheer volume of loans that were being processed.

Fourth and finally, the reduced credit and documentation restrictions and relaxed regulations of subprime lending enabled the creation of numerous alternative loan structures that were convenient and relatively easy to use. The perceived advantages of this factor were that companies could implement the innovation with little effort or cost (furthering profitability), and practitioners and customers would be satisfied with the increased options rather than relying solely on traditional FHA, VA and conventional loans. Moreover, these additional options, as well as improved electronic technology, increased the number and types of opportunities and organizational routines that individuals could quite easily target for potential illicit gain. As such, the flexibility of subprime lending and the ease at which the subprime innovation could be integrated into routine business activities also enabled industry participants to take advantage of these routines to profit from fraudulent transactions. This is consistent with the findings reported by Baker and Faulkner's (2003) that the factors associated with the success of a business' intermediate fraud activities were similar to the factors associated with its success when it was operating legally.

In sum, the subprime innovation and its potential for fraudulent reinvention provided a perceived relative advantage over traditional lending in terms of profitability and target suitability, in terms of increased opportunities for buyers and industry professionals to partake in and take advantage of its legitimate and illegitimate applications with little guardianship, and in ways that did not require much effort. These aspects may have contributed to the conclusions of many potential adopters that the rewards outweighed the risks with respect to both the innovation and its reinvention. These findings are consistent with Routine Activities theory (see Cohen & Felson, 1979) and Rational Choice theory (see Clarke & Cornish, 1985), and they help to explain the rapid rate of adoption in subprime lending and fraud once these advantages started to be realized.

Compatibility

Rogers (2003:240) defines *compatibility* as "the degree to which an innovation is perceived as consistent with the existing values, past experiences, and needs of potential adopters." As noted by the interviewees, this perceived attribute of the subprime innovation actually helps to explain why countless conventional, local, and community banks resisted the opportunity to adopt subprime lending into their niches (at least not right away for a number of them) – it was not perceived as compatible with existing structures or lending strategies. Rogers points out that "an idea that is incompatible with the values and norms of a social system will not be adopted as rapidly as an innovation that is compatible" (p. 15).

Many respondents noted that the subprime concept was not originally received well by traditional lending institutions or finance companies (e.g., community banks; Fannie Mae or Freddie Mac) as it did not fit in well with their existing conservative and lower-risk policies and practices. The factor which seems to have differentiated the adopters from the non-adopters of subprime lending was the perception of how compatible subprime would be with the structure and philosophy (e.g., ethical standards; client targets) of their existing operations.

For example, several practitioners explained that publicly-traded, stockholder-influenced institutions were more likely to take on the subprime (and its associated risk) than the local banks which are frequently expected to reinvest their deposits and profits right back into their own communities. Likewise, larger organizations have greater resources and employ larger numbers of commissioned originators, causing them to be more profit-driven and more likely to have undertaken subprime lending than companies who employed salaried loan officers. This "size" factor was noted as relevant in Weiss' (1997) study of police organization innovativeness; larger organizations were able to undertake and absorb more risk than smaller, resource-challenged departments. An individual's employment status was also noted by several interviewees as a likely contributor to fraud within organizations. Commissioned and sole-proprietor income employees are more dependent on the number and types of transactions they can complete, *however* they get the job done.

To summarize, the perceived compatibility of subprime lending, in terms of values, past experiences, and needs of potential adopters, reflects the priorities and motivations of the parties involved in the mortgage process and helps explain the adoption decision. The respondents noted these same characteristics can also help explain why fraud may have accompanied the subprime product; many claimed that if individuals or their corporate cultures were operating with questionable ethics or morals, or they were previously involved in illegal activities, they may have been more likely to adopt or reinvent the subprime tools for their own material gains.

Complexity

It has been illustrated above that subprime lending was easy to use and exploit by a variety of individuals in and outside of the mortgage industry. This *complexity* characteristic of an innovation is defined as "the degree to which an innovation is perceived as relatively difficult to understand and use" (Rogers, 2003:257). If a product or idea is too complex, it may create a barrier to adoption (it's an inverse relationship), but this does not seem to be the case with subprime lending. It was agreed by the interview participants that the subprime mortgage was not complex, with one alternative product even being called the "Fast & Easy." The variations of subprime mortgages were reportedly easier to use than traditional lending tools for a number of reasons, most notably, due to their no documentation, no verification characteristics.

On the other hand, the complexity of the mortgage process itself may have contributed to the rate (of adoption) and extent of fraud associated with subprime loans. A number of respondents indicated that ill-informed subprime borrowers may have been easier to take advantage of than conventional home buyers. The exorbitant amount of paperwork involved in buying a home and closing a loan is overwhelming for even seasoned borrowers, but being an undereducated, yet proud, borrower makes for a ripe and potentially lucrative opportunity for the motivated offender.

As Benson and Simpson (2009:82) explain, deception "requires a deliberate attempt by one person to mislead another into doing something that they would not do if they had all the facts (i.e., if they hadn't been deceived)." As such, deception requires a deceiver *and* a deceived. It was argued by a number of the study participants that taking advantage of borrower naivety, desperation, and lack of mortgage savvy was a common practice by originators. Other techniques and properties of white collar crime (Benson & Simpson, 2009) are also easy to establish in the provided subprime fraud scenarios. The complexity of the process gave the originator the information advantage over the borrower, which in turn enabled the abuse of trust, and crimes could be concealed without borrower or even underwriter knowledge – all the while appearing to be legitimate.

For reasons outlined above (e.g., high volume of loans, no/low documentation, stated income), parties in subprime transactions were also able to deceive the parties that followed them in the mortgage food chain. For example, by mimicking routine transactions, trust could be abused by passing on fraudulent applications into loans, and ultimately into MBSs, in which defects were concealed (see also Chen, Liao, & Yang, 2008; Hildebrand, 2008), while the information was still within the realm of possibility (e.g., stated income claims). In sum, the *lack* of complexity helps to explain the adoption of subprime lending (consistent with diffusion theory), whereas the *presence* of complexity of the subprime lending and securitization process may have been perceived as a favorable characteristic for partaking in subprime mortgage fraud (consistent with reinvention) as misrepresentations and deception could be concealed.

Trialability

Trialability refers to "the degree to which an innovation may be experimented with on a limited basis" (Rogers, 2003:258). This may involve the temporary use of the complete innovation as presented, trying out its various component parts, or to completely reinventing it. This perceived characteristic of an innovation is also evidenced in the interview transcripts and may help to explain the adoption of both subprime lending and subprime fraud. For example, some respondents noted that loan applications (both legitimate and illegitimate) must be submitted to underwriters, and it was trial and error as to which ones would be accepted and by whom. Individuals were able to test the limits of the available guardianship (as defined by Routine Activities theory; see Cohen & Felson, 1979; Eck & Clarke, 2003), and learned under what conditions they would be positively reinforced for their efforts (consistent with Social Learning Theory; see Burgess & Akers, 1966; Akers, 1990; 1996).

Furthermore, it was noted that established companies could experiment with the subprime products without making any structural changes to their operations. If the trial results were favorable, and the other attributes (e.g., relative advantage, compatibility, complexity) were acceptable, subprime lending might be pursued and operations expanded. Likewise, due to the lack of consequences for submitting fraudulent transactions, subprime fraud could be experimented with prior to any real commitment to crime as a "way of doing business." Therefore, the type of trial and error behavior noted above corresponds well to both decision-making and the adoption rate of subprime lending. It also helps to explain the amount of fraudulent reinvention that has been reported; subprime lending was a loosely-bundled innovation, it was flexible, and it had broad applicability (see Chapter 3).

Observability

"The degree to which the results of an innovation are visible to others" is the final characteristic of an innovation which helps to explain whether an individual decision-making unit adopts and the rate of its adoption, and is referred to as *observability* (Rogers, 2003:258). Consistent with Social Learning Theory (Akers, 1990; 1996) observability taps into the vicarious reinforcement properties which are known to influence cognitions and behavior. Although trialability provides the means in which individuals can experiment with different behaviors (see above), observability does not require active involvement for learning to occur. The observability attributes of subprime lending are most notable in the respondent renditions of how the majority of existing financial institutions (and mortgage practitioners) took a "wait and see" approach with the innovation during the late-1990s and early-2000s. Once these entities witnessed the potential profitability of subprime lending and its ease of use, they were able to make better decisions as to the overall relative advantage, compatibility, complexity, and trialability involved in its adoption.

Rogers (2003) explains that this type of adoption pattern is common; as potential adopters watch the behavior of the earlier adopters, they can make a more informed decision as to whether they should adopt. As Rogers notes, "an individual's actions often depend on a perception of how many other individuals are behaving in a particular way" (Rogers, 2003:349, citing Schelling, 1978). Once again, this innovation characteristic is also consistent with Rational Choice and Social Learning theories (Clarke & Cornish, 1985; Akers, 1990), in that observability establishes the mechanism by which individuals can evaluate their prospective risk/reward ratios in addition to assessing the effort and commitment that might be required to partake in the activity. Several practitioners noted that calculating the profitability of subprime loans was easy as lenders were open about the commission point differentials of various products (e.g., 1-3% for prime, 7-9% for subprime).[39] Or take the situation "when you see another institution shows their fourth-quarter earnings were double yours and you're the same size" (Lender), and you can attribute the difference to subprime lending, you would have benefited from observability.

As compared to subprime lending, the observability characteristic of subprime fraud is a bit less obvious to discern. As with any concealed crime, the degree to which the behavior and results are immediately or outwardly visible to others is rarely going to reach the level at which legitimate behavior is. However, as noted by many of the respondents, after a period of time many in the industry could observe this behavior in mortgage processing and they learned what types of actions crossed the line from unethical to illegal, what types of

---

[39] Baker & Faulkner (2003) argued that scarcity and competition may actually impede the willingness of investors to share or make visible the results (benefits) of their opportunities. According to respondents, this does not appear to be the case with subprime lending, as: (1) depository institutions must keep their "books" open to inspection; and, (2) there was plenty of business to go around when the market was escalating the way it did.

fraudulent activities were being practiced and by whom, as well as what the potential risks and rewards of the behavior were.

Some interviewees also insisted that many mortgage occupation newcomers were socialized directly into fraudulent business cultures, either by co-workers or by industry associates who would have provided these new practitioners with untold opportunities to observe fraudulent behavior and the potential benefits of participating in subprime fraud (see also Ashforth & Anand, 2003). This last factor is consistent with the precepts of Differential Association theory as discussed by Sutherland (1983).

In conclusion, observability was present with both subprime lending and subprime fraud, but in different ways. Practitioners were able to consider the results of both types of behavior as they went about their respective occupational and organizational routines. According to the respondents, this innovation characteristic was a factor in the decision of countless traditional institutions to enter the subprime market, and for countless individuals and organizations to participate in subprime fraud. Besides factoring into the innovation adoption decision, this attribute, or the ability of decision-making units to observe the results of earlier adopters, also helps to explain the timing of the critical mass timeframes and the speed at which subprime originations and subprime fraud escalated from those points forward.

Summary

The respondents substantiated that the attributes of subprime lending were communicated primarily through formal and informal government, industry, and media channels, whereas perceptions of the subprime fraud characteristics were more likely to be cultivated through observation of their informal occupational, organizational, or industry associations. This is consistent with the findings of Snyder et al. (2009) in their examination of CEO stock option backdating. In conclusion, from the practitioner's perspectives, elements of these innovation characteristics help explain the persuasion stage of the subprime lending and subprime fraud innovation-decision processes (see Figure 4.1), the rate of adoption of the subprime lending innovation, and the spread of its subsequent fraudulent reinvention.

Yet these very same characteristics are evident in the demise of subprime lending, which illustrates the somewhat cyclical nature of decision-making. In the spirit of fiscal accountability and financial rationality, one might assume that the growth in fraud reporting over the years following the critical mass point (from 2003 forward) might have at the same time stymied the growth in subprime lending (demonstrated above), but it was not until mid-2007 that the financial markets actually put the brakes on subprime lending. This reverse "tipping point," or the point at which individual adopters discontinued use of the subprime lending tool (voluntarily and involuntarily), is consistent with Rogers' (2003) explanation of "disenchantment discontinuance" in which the decision to reject a previously adopted idea is made due to the poor performance of the innovation (it has lost its perceptual advantage). In defense of the industry, the poor performance of subprime and other mortgage products (e.g., high default rates, inflated property and securities values, unstable economy, unprecedented levels of fraud, etc.) may not have been practically observable and completely understood until this later time.

CHAPTER 10

Discussion and Future Directions

Applicability of Diffusion Theory to Criminology and Criminal Justice

As argued in prior chapters, although the opportunity perspective of white collar crime is gaining momentum in criminological thought and discourse, the underlying *legitimate* opportunity structures and processes which actually stimulate and facilitate these new types of offenses are not well understood. As Friedrichs (2010:628) notes, "mortgage origination can range from purely legitimate to purely illegitimate and everywhere in between." Despite this insight, how potential offenders learn of newly formed legitimate business opportunities to even be able to take advantage of them is not well explained or accounted for by any one or combination of criminological theories.[40] As stated in the introductory chapter, a primary purpose of this study is to contribute to the field's understanding of white collar crime opportunity structures by demonstrating how and why legal and illegal practices spread throughout the mortgage industry over time through the interpretive framework of diffusion of innovations theory (Rogers, 2003). In the paragraphs that follow, it is argued that the diffusion of innovations perspective, as illustrated throughout this study, provides demonstrable adjunct advantages to criminological theory, white collar crime research, and crime prevention and control policy.

It has been argued that the theories of Differential Association, Routine Activities, Social Learning, and Rational Choice, and the situational crime prevention and opportunity perspectives offer varying degrees of insight into the phenomenon of white collar crime. It is becoming increasingly understood that a significant contributor to all types of criminal events is opportunity, and although each of these theories/perspectives approaches opportunity in a unique manner, they are inconsistent with respect to the importance of this fundamental element of crime. Although promising theorizing is beginning to appear, especially with respect to the situational crime prevention and white collar crime opportunity perspectives (see e.g., Clarke, 1999; Benson & Madensen, 2007; Benson, Madensen & Eck, 2009; Benson & Simpson, 2009), none of these theories or perspectives provides an established assemblage of components capable of explaining how new opportunities for legitimate and illegitimate activities originate or traverse throughout a business system. As demonstrated herein, the diffusion framework may provide this missing linkage by accounting for the development of innovative crime opportunities.

Furthermore, similar to Differential Association (Sutherland, 1983) and Social Learning Theory (Akers, 1990), diffusion theory is grounded in the understanding that human behavior is learned through associations and communications with others, and that behavior is

---

[40] However, see the criminological theory discussion in Chapter 3 in which legal and illegal behaviors are attributed to the same type of cognitive processes (e.g., Social Learning, Differential Association).

capable of changing over time (e.g., how later adopters have changed their views on an opportunity's advantages). Also, as demonstrated with subprime lending and subprime fraud, certain communication channels and associations, and the perceived characteristics of ideas (or tangible items or processes) are more likely than others to influence decision-making and behavior. This in turn helps to explain why some members of a social system may choose to take advantage of opportunities earlier than others, or never at all (legitimate or otherwise).

According to diffusion theory, and substantiated empirically through hundreds of multi-disciplinary studies (see Rogers, 2003), when a new idea (or product) is presented to a business system the idea travels through the system in a generally expected manner. The subprime mortgage innovation and its subsequent reinvention appear to have followed this traditional pattern based on the characteristics that contributed to the adopters' innovation-decision process as well as to their resulting rates of adoption. As such, in utilizing diffusion theory to interpret the crime of subprime mortgage fraud, it was demonstrated that the spread of new opportunities for white collar crime may be more predictable than what has been previously assumed. If this is the case, and white collar criminal opportunities are eventually confirmed to diffuse (as innovations or reinventions) in the same way as legitimate opportunities (albeit with differing characteristic weights and conditions), various criminological perspectives may be capable of further theoretical advancement with respect to new types of crime. These advancements can be assisted by diffusion of innovations theory, and the precise mechanisms for the "diffusion of illegal practices" (Sutherland, 1983) may finally be able to be more explicitly conceptualized.

In addition to the theoretical advancements diffusion theory may ultimately provide to criminology, the diffusion framework has been shown herein and by others (see e.g., Baker & Faulkner, 2003; Snyder et al., 2009) to provide a valuable interpretive framework with which to approach the study of white collar crime. It does so by outlining a multitude of variables associated with the spread of new ideas and opportunities throughout a social system, and is sufficiently flexible to enable these variables and constructs to be operationalized according to the nature of the system and behavioral phenomena under study. No other single theory seems to provide this breadth or flexibility for research within one perspective; a practical consideration which may help to facilitate a more methodical approach to the study of white collar crime opportunities, especially in light of the trend to create typologies in white collar crime research.

And finally, as is a common concern in white collar crime prevention and control efforts, attempts to limit opportunities for crime may also limit new and existing opportunities for legitimate business operations. For example, as discussed by some of the interviewees, the mortgage market is so "tight" right now that it may actually be inhibiting its own ability to heal. By restricting the qualifications of borrowers, and increasing the regulations for lenders, the housing market, although showing signs of limited improvement in some areas, remains largely stagnant with too much inventory on hand. The changes that have been made, however, appear consistent with the basic tenets of situational crime prevention – that is, if you cannot change the disposition of the offender, the opportunities or rewards for offending must be reduced and/or the risk of being caught or sanctions must be increased (Clarke, 1980).

As revealed in the practitioner interviews, the opportunity for mortgage fraud has always and will continue to exist. The subprime mortgage products and processes that were made available in the 1990s, however, increased the population of potential offenders, increased temptation and suitable targets, and increased the ease at which motivated individuals could take advantage of the opportunities to commit crime. As such, it was not necessarily the existing routines of the housing/mortgage industry that were problematic, it was the actual type of subprime "products" that created an environment rich with white collar crime motivation and opportunity. The relevance of this finding is that in order to understand how to control a potentially criminogenic product or process (to reduce crime opportunities), the product and the process by which it is expected to spread through a business system must first be understood. This also suggests that the financial industry must maintain responsibility for its own crime "prevention" in terms of how it originates and structures its innovations (e.g., advantages, risk, ability to be reinvented) and how it facilitates or encourages the innovations' eventual diffusions. As demonstrated herein with subprime mortgage fraud, diffusion theory can be utilized effectively to contribute to this understanding.

Future Research

Both the results and limitations of this study present directions for future research, particularly with respect to sampling, methodology, and the utilization of diffusion of innovations theory. First: *sampling*. The small, non-random, convenience sample used here could be improved on with a larger national random sample of mortgage industry practitioners so that the demographic, occupational and geographic characteristics of the sample would be more representative and the results more generalizable. On the other hand, a purposive sampling of industry practitioners who have been accused/convicted of white collar crime associated with the subprime market could be utilized. This latter approach would possibly bring more enlightenment into the rationalizations and neutralizations used to support their illegal behavior. Ensuring representation from the offender population, or combining each of these types of study participants, would also allow for a more in-depth examination of contextual, demographic or dispositional correlates of their respective behaviors.

Second: *methodology*. The type of qualitative research conducted here could be used as a conduit for a survey of the mortgage industry which would allow for a quantitative analysis of practitioner decision-making, of the subprime innovation and its diffusion, as well as its reinvention. This would also improve on the internal and external validity of the results.

Third: *diffusion of innovations*. Criminal theory and criminal justice researchers would benefit from becoming familiar with the diffusion perspective and to investigate its use further. It has been repeatedly mentioned herein that the multi-disciplinary framework has established and widespread theoretical and empirical applications. As such, it demonstrates potential for examining not only new types of white collar crimes, but other offenses that have temporal and spatial qualities, as well as for examining the adoption and reinvention of laws, policies, and practices throughout and across the criminal justice system.

Concluding Remarks

Even though the entrance of borrowers, lenders, and investors into the high-risk subprime mortgage market may have appeared to represent economic rationality, it has been discussed throughout this monograph that this collective action may have ultimately resulted in widespread fiscal irrationality, and contributed to the abrupt decline of subprime feasibility within just a few short years. The detriment this product caused to the quality of exchange relationships, as well as to the financial stability of individuals and communities, was caused not only by across-the-board fiscal irresponsibility (e.g., inattention to risk; permissible but predatory-type lending), but according to industry practitioners, by the unprecedented display and spread of greed and criminal behavior (e.g., loan application misrepresentations via lying and deceit). This behavior may have not been intended or anticipated by the originators or supporters of subprime lending, but as demonstrated herein the innovation's design allowed industry practitioners and borrowers to take advantage of it in a variety of unintended and illegal ways.

Subprime lending and its associated fraud provided a relevant phenomenon with which to examine the compatibility of the diffusion perspective and conventional criminological theory. This study has attempted to establish the viability of diffusion theory specifically to the examination and interpretation of new types of white collar crime opportunities, and more generally to other areas of interest in criminology and criminal justice. If the results reported herein are any indication of the utility of the diffusion framework to guide and interpret criminal events and behavior, especially with respect to the role of opportunity, then this mission has been accomplished. As "emerging fraud trends" continue to challenge and drain law enforcement resources (FBI, 2010b), further exploration of how and why these trends and new white collar crime opportunities form and diffuse is paramount to the future of our nation's security and economic stability.

APPENDIX A

Interview Guide

During the course of the interview, ask the respondent to address the following questions:

1. Please tell me your employment status and give me an idea of your primary job responsibilities.
2. Why, when, and how was subprime lending originally devised and presented to the financial community, and explain the parties who have been involved in its use?
3. What characteristics of the subprime lending innovation may have contributed to its rate and extent of adoption?
4. What types of fraud have been associated with subprime lending, and what characteristics of subprime lending do you believe contributed to this fraud?
5. Are there characteristics of subprime lending which make it more likely to be used for fraudulent purposes than other mortgage tools and techniques (e.g., prime loans)? Please explain.

6. What communication channels (e.g., formal or informal) have been most likely to diffuse the legitimate as compared to the illegitimate applications of the innovation?
7. What types of regulatory controls could have been implemented to reduce the fraud associated with subprime lending; and can these controls still be introduced to prevent further fraud?

GUIDE & PROMPTS

Use the following sections as a topic guide for further information as time permits.

Familiarize yourself with the following prompts. Use the prompts if necessary, and encourage elaboration on any other applicable or pertinent points made during the interview.

I. Participant Employment Status and Job Responsibilities

- What is your current occupation and job title?
- Are you independent or an employee of a company?
- What is the primary business of your company?
- How long have you been employed in this position with this company?
- Please outline your work experience in the mortgage (or other) industry prior to being employed in your current position.
- Please list your primary job responsibilities.
- In what capacity do you serve the clientele of your company?
- What other types of mortgage service providers do you communicate and/or collaborate with on a regular basis?
- On average, how many contacts with clients and other mortgage service providers do you have in a regular week?
- What does a typical day at work look like for you?

II. The Subprime Mortgage (SPM) and its History

- Please explain the basic process and life of an SPM (from the original application, appraisal and documentation activities, through loan processing, all the way through the bundling and sales of mortgage-backed securities).

- What are the core elements of the SPM (i.e., the features that are responsible for its effectiveness)?
- Do you know when (approximate year) the SPM first came into existence?
- An innovation can be defined as "an idea, practice, or object that is perceived as new by an individual or other unit of adoption." In this case the innovation is the SPM and the unit of adoption is the mortgage/financial industry. In your view, was the SPM option considered to be an innovation by the mortgage/financial industry at that time?
- Was the SPM created through some type of governmental program or action?
- Please explain your understanding of who (e.g., agency) originally conceived of and formulated the SPM.
- What was the stimulus for the SPM (e.g., why was it originally designed as a lending option)?
- Specifically, what needs was the tool designed to meet (for the community, individual borrowers, lenders, financial industry, etc.)?
- How did the SPM innovation/tool augment or complement other mortgage lending and investment tools and strategies at the time?
- What types of lenders or mortgage service providers were originally eligible to use the SPM? Were there stipulations or limitations on its use?
- What types of regulations originally accompanied the use of the SPM? Please explain.

III. Subprime Mortgage Diffusion

- Do you recall when you first learned about the SPM?
- By what communication channels did you first learn about SPMs (e.g., in school, a conference presentation, training seminar, from coworkers, from contacts in the mortgage field, through the media)?

- By what means was the information communicated to you (e.g., verbally, written, casual conversation, group presentation, training manual, etc.)?
- Would you define these channels and means of communication as formal or informal?
- Do you believe others in the industry also learned of SPMs through this type of communication? During the same rough time period?
- By what other channels or means was SPM information presented to the financial community?
- How long (by what year) would you estimate it took for the SPM to become a standard tool across the United States mortgage industry?
- Are there other characteristics of the SPM that may help to explain either the rate or extent of its adoption?

IV. SPM Adopters

- Did all eligible financial industry professionals and/or businesses begin using the SPM when it first became available, or did some wait a period of time to use it even though they were originally eligible?
- What characteristics of financial industry professionals and/or businesses might
- help to explain why they chose to adopt, reject, delay, or discontinue the use of SPMs when they did?

V. Opportunity Structure of the Subprime Mortgage

- Was the use of SBMs originally confined to certain types of lenders or to certain areas of the country?
- Did the original stipulations or regulations of the SPM (which you identified previously) limit the availability or viability of the subprime option to certain types or sizes of companies/businesses?
- What were the original and general criteria that both lenders and borrowers were expected to meet to utilize the SPM?

- Did the advent or spread of the SPM itself create opportunities for new types of businesses or mortgage service providers? New occupations for individuals? Please explain.
- Were criteria changed at some point to allow new parties to enter the SPM business? How so?
- At what point (approximate year) did these new entities enter the mortgage industry?
- Are there currently restrictions on who can utilize SPMs or is anyone involved in traditional mortgage servicing allowed to use them? Please explain.

VI. Reinvention

- Is the SPM process, as you explain it today, consistent with your original understanding of the tool, or did the process evolve over the years?
- Have the core elements of the SPM (as you defined previously) changed since it was first introduced? In what ways?
- If major changes have occurred, what stimulated these changes?
- What characteristics of the SPM made it possible to alter its core elements? Please explain.
- Did you learn about these characteristics and potential alterations when you first learned of the SPM itself, or was there a lag between first knowledge and subsequent knowledge? What was the lag time?
- By what communication channels did you first learn about SPM alterations (e.g., in school, a conference presentation, training seminar, from coworkers, from contacts in the mortgage field, through the media)?
- By what means was the information communicated to you (e.g., verbally, written, casual conversation, group presentation, training manual, etc.)?
- Would you define these channels and means of communication as formal or informal?

- Do you believe others in the industry also learned of potential SPM alterations through this type of communication? During the same rough time period?
- By what other channels or means was the issue of SPM alterations originally presented to the financial community?
- At some point, were the original criteria revised to allow further expansion of SPM use by lenders/mortgage service providers? Who was responsible for reducing these limitations?
- Did the original expectations or regulations apply to these newcomers, or were policies revised over the years? Why and how so?
- What types of regulatory controls were or could have been applied to the original SPM core elements to minimize the potential for its alteration?

VII. Fraud

- Do you recall when you first learned about fraud in the SPM?
- Did you gain knowledge about the SPM and SPM fraud simultaneously or was there a lag between your first knowledge of the SPM and SPM fraud?
- By what communication channels did you first learn about SPM fraud (e.g., in school, a conference presentation, training seminar, from coworkers, from contacts in the mortgage field, through the media)?
- By what means was the information communicated to you (e.g., verbally, written, casual conversation, group presentation, training manual, etc.)?
- Would you define these channels and means of communication as formal or informal?
- Do you believe others in the industry also learned of SPM fraud through this type of communication? During the same rough time period?
- By what other channels or means was the issue of SPM fraud originally presented to the financial community?

- Would you say that the channels communicating the legitimate use of the SPM were the same or different from the channels communicating its illegitimate use? Please explain.
- Was the problem of SBM fraud originally confined to certain types of lenders or to certain areas of the country? Please explain.
- How long (by what year) would you estimate it took for SPM fraud to become a standard occurrence in the mortgage industry?
- Please explain how and what types of fraud or other corrupt practices can occur with respect to the SPM.
- Returning to the list of characteristics of innovations that are generally associated with their rate and extent of adoption, which, if any, of these characteristics of the SPM may have appealed to financial industry professionals that might help to explain the speed at which fraud spread?
- Which of these characteristics of the SPM may have appealed to financial industry professionals that might help to explain the extent of fraud (the breadth of its use)?
- Are there other characteristics of the SPM that may help to explain either the rate or extent of SPM fraud?
- Are there characteristics of the SPM that make it more or less likely to be re- invented for fraudulent purposes than the characteristics of other mortgage tools and techniques (e.g., prime loans)? What are these?
- Do any of the adopter characteristics apply to financial industry professionals and/or businesses involved in fraud and which help to explain the time to their involvement in fraudulent activities?
- What other characteristics of financial industry professionals might help to explain their involvement in, their time to involvement in, or the overall prevalence or incidence of, SPM fraud? What types of regulatory controls were or could have been applied to the original SPM or its alterations to minimize the potential of its use for fraudulent purposes?

VIII. Wrap-Up

- Is there anything you would like to clarify with respect to anything we discussed today?
- Is there anything else you would like to add?

References

Aalbers, M. B. (2009). Wrong assumptions in the financial crisis. *Critical Perspectives on International Business*, 5:94-97.

Agnew, R. (1994). The techniques of neutralization and violence. *Criminology*, 32:555-580.

Akers, R. L. (1990). Rational choice, deterrence, and social learning theory in criminology: The path not taken. *Journal of Criminal Law & Criminology*, 81:653-676.

Akers, R. L. (1996). Is differential association/social learning cultural deviance theory? *Criminology*, 34:229-247.

Apgar, W. C., & Herbert, C. E. (2006). *Subprime lending and alternative financial service providers: A literature review and empirical analysis.* Prepared for U.S. Department of Housing and Urban Development Office of Policy Development and Research. Cambridge, MA: Abt Associates Inc.

Archer, W. R., Ling, D. C., & McGill, G. A. (2003). Household income, termination risk and mortgage pricing. *Journal of Real Estate Finance and Economics*, 27:111-138.

Ashforth, B. E., & Anand, V. (2003). The normalization of corruption in organizations. *Research in Organizational Behavior*, 25:1-52.

Ashforth, B. E., Gioia, D. A., Robinson, S. L., & Trevino, L. K. (2008). Reviewing organizational corruption. *Academy of Management Review*, 33:670-684.

Baker, W. E., & Faulkner, R. R. (2003). Diffusion of fraud: Intermediate economic crime and investor dynamics. *Criminology*, 41:1173-1206.

Barlow, H. D. (1993). From fiddle factors to networks of collusion: Charting the waters of small business crime. *Crime, Law, and Social Change*, 20:319-337.

Barr, A. (2007). S&P may downgrade $12 billion of subprime securities. *MarketWatch*, July 10, 2007.

Beken, T. V., & Balcaen, A. (2006). Crime opportunities provided by legislation in market sectors: mobile phones, waste disposal, banking, pharmaceuticals. *European Journal on Criminal Policy and Research*, 12:299-323.

Benson, M. L. (1985). Denying the guilty mind: Accounting for involvement in a white-collar crime. *Criminology*, 23:583-607.

Benson, M. L., & Cullen, F. T. (1998). *Combating corporate crime: Local prosecutors at work*. Boston: Northeastern University.

Benson, M. L. & Madensen, T. D. (2006). Situational crime prevention and White-collar crime. In Henry N. Pontell and Gilbert Geis (Eds.), *International handbook of white-collar and corporate crime*, (pp. 609-626). Dordrecht, The Netherlands: Kluwer Academic/Plenum.

Benson, M. L., Madensen, T. D., & Eck, J. E. (2009). White-collar crime from an opportunity perspective. In Sally S. Simpson and David Weisburd (Eds.), *The criminology of white-collar crime*, (pp. 175-193). Verlag: Springer.

Benson, M. L., & Simpson, S. S. (2009). *White-Collar crime: An opportunity perspective*. New York: Routledge.

Berente, N., Yoo, Y., & Lyytinen, K. (2008). Measuring distributed innovation. *Academy of Management Annual Meeting*, Anaheim, CA; August, 2008.

Bitner, R. (2008). *Confessions of a subprime lender: An insider's tale of greed, fraud, and ignorance*. Hoboken, NJ: John Wiley & Sons.

Bouffard, J.A. (2007). Predicting differences in the perceived relevance of crime's costs and benefits in a test of rational choice theory. *International Journal of Offender Therapy and Comparative Criminology*, 51:461-485.

Braithwaite, J. (1985). White-collar crime. *American Review of Sociology*, 11:1-25.

Burgess, R. L., & Akers, R. L. (1966). A differential association-reinforcement theory of criminal behavior. *Social Problems*, 14:128-147.

CBS (2008). House Of Cards: The Mortgage Mess. 60 Minutes Reports on How the Subprime Loan Crisis is Shaking Markets Worldwide. May 25, 2008. Available at: http://www.cbsnews.com/stories/2008/01/25/60minutes/main3752515.shtml. *CBS Interactive Inc.*

Calem, P. S., Gillen, K., & Wachter, S. (2004). The neighborhood distribution of subprime mortgage lending. *Journal of Real Estate Finance and Economics*, 29:393-410.

Carswell, A. T., & Bachtel, D. C. (2007). Mortgage fraud: White-collar crime with long- standing community effects. *Public Administration and Management: An Interactive Journal*, 12:39-69.

Chen, R-R., Liao, H-H., & Yang, T. T. (2008). Market risk of mortgage-backed securities with consistent measures. *Journal of Real Estate Finance and Economics*, 36:121-140.

Chomsisengphet, S., & Pennington-Cross, A. (2006). The evolution of the subprime mortgage market. *Federal Reserve Bank of St. Louis Review*, January/February 2006, 88(1):31-56.

Clark, M. S., & Mills, J. (1993). The difference between communal and exchange relationships: What it is and is not. *Personality and Social Psychology Bulletin*, 19: 684-691.

Clarke, R. V. (1980). "Situational" crime prevention: Theory and practice. *British Journal of Criminology*, 20: 136-147.

Clarke, R. V. (1999). The theory and practice of situational crime prevention. *Rutgers University School of Criminal Justice*. Retrieved on July 1, 2010 from: www.e- doca.eu/content/docs/Situational_crime_prevention.pdf.

Clarke, R. V., & Cornish, D. B. (1985). Modeling offenders' decisions: A framework for research and policy. *Crime and Justice*, 6:147-185.

Clarke, R. V., & Cornish, D. B. (2001). Rational choice. In Paternoster, R., and Bachman, R. (Eds.), *Explaining criminals and crime: Essays in contemporary criminological theory*, (pp.23-42). Los Angeles: Roxbury.

Clinard, M. B. & Quinney, R. (1973). *Criminal behavior systems: A typology, 2nd Ed.* New York: Holt, Rinehart & Winston.

Clinard, M. B., & Yeager, P. C. (1978). Corporate crime: Issues in research. *Criminology*, 16:255-272.

Cohen, L. E., & Felson, M. (1979). Social change and crime rate trends: A routine activities approach. *American Sociological Review*, 44:588-608.

Cohen, J., & Tita, G. (1999). Diffusion in homicide: Exploring a general method for detecting spatial diffusion processes. *Journal of Quantitative Criminology*, 15:451-493.

Coleman, J. W. (1987). Toward an integrated theory of white-collar crime. *American Journal of Sociology*, 93:406-439.

Coleman, J., Katz, E., & Menzel, H. (1957). The diffusion of an innovation among physicians. *Sociometry*, 20:253-270.

Cornish, D. B., & Clarke, R. V. (1987). Understanding crime displacement: An application of rational choice theory. *Criminology*, 25:933-947.

Cornish, D. B., & Clarke, R. V. (2003). Opportunities, precipitators and criminal decisions: A reply to Wortley's critique of situational crime prevention. *Crime Prevention Studies*, 16:41-96.

Courchane, M. J., Surette, B. J., & Zorn, P. M. (2004). Subprime borrowers: Mortgage transitions and outcomes. *Journal of Real Estate Finance and Economics*, 29:365-392.

Cressey, D. R. (1989). The poverty of theory in corporate crime research. In William S. Laufer and Freda Adler (Eds.), *Advances in criminological theory, Vol. 1*, (pp. 31-55). New Brunswick: Transaction.

Cullen, F. T., & Agnew, R. (2002). *Criminological theory: Past to present (Essential readings)*. Los Angeles: Roxbury.

Davis, E. P., & Karim, D. (2008). Could early warning systems have helped to predict the sub-prime crisis? *National Institute Economic Review*, 206:35-47.

Demyanyk, Y. S. (2009). Quick exits of subprime mortgages. *Federal Reserve Bank of St. Louis Review*, March/April, 2009, 91(2):79-93.

Diamond, Jr., A. M. (2003). Edwin Mansfield's contributions to the economics of technology. *Research Policy*, 32:1607-1617.

Eck, J., & Clarke, R. V. (2003). Classifying common police problems: A routine activity approach. *Crime Prevention Studies*, 16:7-39.

Edelhertz, H. (1970). Selected chapters from: *The nature, impact, and prosecution of white- collar crime*. Washington, D.C.: U. S. Department of Justice.

Fannie Mae (2006). *Fannie Mae mortgage fraud update*. Available at https://www.efanniemae.com/utility/legal/antifraud.jsp.

Fannie Mae (2009). *Fannie Mae mortgage fraud update*. Available at https://www.efanniemae.com/utility/legal/antifraud.jsp.

Fannie Mae (2010). *Fannie Mae mortgage fraud update*. Available at https://www.efanniemae.com/utility/legal/antifraud.jsp.

Federal Bureau of Investigation (FBI) (2010). Available at http://www.fbi.gov/hq/mortgage_fraud.htm. Last visited on March 17, 2010.

Federal Bureau of Investigation (FBI) (2010b). *2009 Mortgage fraud report "Year in review."* Retrieved July 1, 2010 from: http://www.fbi.gov/publications/fraud/mortgage_fraud09.htm#3.

Federal Bureau of Investigation (FBI) (2011). *2010 Mortgage fraud report "Year in review."* Retrieved March 22. 2012 from: FBI.gov.

Federal Bureau of Investigation (FBI) (2012). *Just the Facts: Mortgage Fraud Statistics*. Retrieved March 22, 2012 from: FBI.gov.

Felson, M. (2001). The routine activity approach: A very versatile theory of crime. In Raymond Paternoster and Ronet Bachman (Eds.), *Explaining criminals and crime: Essays in contemporary criminological theory*, (pp. 43-46). Los Angeles: Roxbury.

Fifth Third Bank. (2010). *Group 1 Rate Sheet – FL. Fifth Third wholesale lending news: Week Of 07/05/10*. Fifth Third Bancorp. Retrieved on July 8, 2010 from: https://www.53.com.

Financial Crimes Enforcement Network (FinCEN). (2006). *Mortgage loan fraud: An industry assessment based upon suspicious activity report analysis*. U.S. Department of Treasury, Regulatory Policy and Programs Division, November 2006.

Financial Crimes Enforcement Network (FinCEN). (2006b). *The SAR activity review: Trends, tips & issues. Issue 16: October 2009*. U.S. Department of Treasury, Regulatory Policy and Programs Division.

Financial Crimes Enforcement Network (FinCEN). (2009). *The SAR activity review: Trends, tips & issues. Issue 10: May 2006.* U.S. Department of Treasury, Regulatory Policy and Programs Division.

Financial Crimes Enforcement Network (FinCEN). (2009b). *Filing trends in mortgage loan fraud: A review of Suspicious Activity Reports filed July 1, 2007 through June 30, 2008.* U.S. Department of Treasury, Regulatory Policy and Programs Division.

Financial Crimes Enforcement Network (FinCEN). (2010). *Mortgage loan fraud update: Suspicious activity report filings in 3rd quarter 2011.* U.S. Department of Treasury, Regulatory Policy and Programs Division.

Financial Crimes Enforcement Network (FinCEN). (2012). *The SAR Activity Review – By the Numbers: Issue 14 (June 2010).* U.S. Department of Treasury, Regulatory Policy and Programs Division.

Foote, C. L., Gerardi, K., Goette, L., & Willen, P.S. (2008). Just the facts: An initial analysis of subprime's role in the housing crisis. *Journal of Housing Economics*, 17:291-305.

Frame, W. S., & White, L. J. (2009). Technological change, financial innovation, and diffusion in banking. *Federal Reserve Bank of Atlanta*: Working Paper Series 2009-10.

Friedrichs, D. O. (2007). *Trusted criminals: White-collar crime in contemporary society, 3rd Ed.* Belmont, CA: Wadsworth.

Friedrichs, D. O. (2010). Mortgage origination fraud and the global economic crisis: incremental versus transformative policy initiatives. *Criminology & Public Policy*, 9:627-632.

Gabaix, X., Krishnamurthy, A., & Vigneron, O. (2007). Limits of arbitrage: Theory and evidence from the mortgage-backed securities market. *The Journal of Finance*, 62:557-595.

Geis, G. & Goff, C. (1983). Introduction. In E. H. Sutherland, *White-collar crime: The uncut version.* London: Yale University Press.

Geis, G., Meier, R. F., & Salinger, L. M. (1995). *White-collar crime: Classic and contemporary views, 3rd Ed.* New York: Free Press.

Glaeser, E. L., & Kallal, H. D. (1997). Thin markets, asymmetric information, and mortgage-backed securities. *Journal of Financial Intermediation*, 6:64-86.

Grabosky, P., & Shover, N. (2010). Forestalling the next epidemic of white-collar crime: Linking policy to theory. *Criminology & Public Policy*, 9:641-654.

Gramlich. E. M. (2007). *America's second housing boom*. Washington, DC: The Urban Institute: Opportunity and Ownership Project.

Haider, M., & Kreps, G. L. (2004). Forty years of diffusion of innovations: Utility and value in public health. *Journal of Health Communication*, 9:3-11.

Hays, S. P. (1996). Influences on reinvention during the diffusion of innovations. *Political Research Quarterly*, 49:631-650.

Heuson, A., Passmore, W., & Sparks, R. (2001). Credit scoring and mortgage securitization: Implications for mortgage rates and credit availability. *Journal of Real Estate Finance and Economics*, 23:337-363.

Hildebrand, P. M. (2008). The subprime crisis: A central banker's perspective. *Journal of Financial Stability*, 4:313-320.

Hirschi, T. & Gottfredson, M. (1987). Causes of white-collar crime. *Criminology*, 25:949-974.

Hornick, R. (2004). Some reflections on diffusion theory and the role of Everett Rogers. *Journal of Health Communication*, 9:143-148.

Immergluck, D., & Smith, G. (2005). Measuring the effect of subprime lending on neighborhood foreclosures: Evidence from Chicago. *Urban Affairs Review*, 40:362-389.

Internal Revenue Service (IRS) (2010). Located at *IRS.gov*. Last visited on March 24, 2012.

Kincaid, D. L. (2004). From innovation to social norm: Bounded normative influence. *Journal of Health Communication*, 9:37-57.

King, W. R. (2000). Measuring police innovation: issues and measurement. *Policing: An International Journal of Police Strategies & Management*, 23:303-317.

Kuhn, T. S. (1996). *The structure of scientific revolutions, 3rd Ed.* Chicago: University of Chicago Press.

Lacoste, J., & Tremblay, P. (2003). Crime and innovation: A script analysis of patterns in check forgery. *Crime Prevention Studies*, 16:169-196.

Lander, G. H., Barker, K., Zabelina, M., & Williams, T. A. (2009). Subprime mortgage tremors: An international issue. *International Atlantic Economic Society*, 15:1-16.

Levi, M. (2008). Organized fraud and organizing frauds: Unpacking research on networks and organization. *Criminology & Criminal Justice*, 8:389-419.

Mahajan, V., & Peterson, R. A. (1985). *Models for innovation diffusion.* Beverly Hills: Sage.

Mansfield, E. (1961). Technical change and the rate of imitation. *Econometrics*, 29:741-766.

Matsueda, R. L. (1988). The current state of differential association theory. *Crime & Delinquency*, 34:277-306.

Mayer, C. J., & Pence, K. (2008). Subprime mortgages: What, where, and to whom? NBER Working paper Series, Working Paper 14083. *National Bureau of Economic Research.* Retrieved on July 1, 2010 from: http://www.nber.org/papers/w14083. © 2008 by Christopher J. Mayer and Karen Pence.

Meyer, G. (2004). Diffusion methodology: Time to innovate? *Journal of Health Communication*, 9:59-69.

Mooney, C. Z., & Lee, M-H. (1999). Morality policy reinvention: State death penalties. *ANNALS of the American Academy of Political and Social Science*, 566:80-92.

Mortgage Asset Research Institute (MARI) (2006). *Eighth periodic mortgage fraud report to Mortgage Bankers Association.* Reston, VA: Mortgage Asset Research Institute, Inc. LexisNexis.

Mortgage Asset Research Institute (MARI) (2009). *Eleventh periodic mortgage fraud report to Mortgage Bankers Association.* Reston, VA: Mortgage Asset Research Institute, Inc. LexisNexis.

Mortgage Asset Research Institute (MARI) (2010). *Twelfth periodic mortgage fraud report to Mortgage Bankers Association.* LexisNexis Mortgage Asset Research Institute, Inc. Reston, VA: LexisNexis.

Mortgage Asset Research Institute (MARI) (2011). *Thirteenth periodic mortgage fraud case report.* Reston, VA: Mortgage Asset Research Institute, Inc. LexisNexis.

Nagin, D. S., & Paternoster, R. (1993). Enduring individual differences and rational choice theories of crime. *Law & Society Review*, 27, 467-496.

National White-Collar Crime Center. (2008). *Mortgage fraud.* Available at: www.nw3c.org.

NY.gov: New York State (2010). September 21, 2010 Press release: District Attorney Vance announces sentencing in $100 million mortgage fraud case. Retrieved on February 13, 2012 from: http://www.dfs.ny.gov/about/press/pr100921.htm.

Nguyen, T. H. (2011). *Fraud and the subprime mortgage crisis.* El Paso, TX: LFB Scholarly.

Nguyen, T. H., & Pontell, H. N. (2010). Mortgage origination fraud and the global economic crisis: A criminological analysis. *Criminology & Public Policy*, 9:591-612.

Oxford English Dictionary (2008). Available at: http://www.oed.com/news/updates/newwords0806.html. Last visited on May 19, 2010.

Pankratz, M., Hallfors, D., & Cho, H. (2002). Measuring perceptions of innovation adoption: the diffusion of a federal drug prevention policy. *Health Education Research*, 17:315-326.

Patterson, L. A., & Koller, C. A. (2011). Diffusion of fraud through subprime lending: The perfect storm. In Mathieu Deflem (Ed.) *Sociology of Crime, Law and deviance: Economic Crisis and Crime*, 16:25-45. Bingley, UK: Emerald.

Pavlov, A. D. (2001). Competing risks of mortgage termination: Who refinances, who moves, and who defaults? *Journal of Real Estate Finance and Economics*, 23:185-211.

Piliavin, I., Gartner, R., Thornton, C., & Matsueda, R. L. (1986). Crime, deterrence, and rational choice. *American Sociological Review*, 51:101-119.

Pontell, H. N., & Calavita, K. (1990). "Heads I win, tails you lose": Deregulation, crime, and crisis in the savings and loan industry. *Crime & Delinquency*, 36:309-341.

Posavac, R. J., & Carey, R. G. (2007). *Program evaluation: Methods and case studies, 7th Ed.* Upper Saddle River, New Jersey: Pearson Prentice Hall.

QSR International. (2010). *NVivo.* Available at: http://www.qsrinternational.com/default.aspx.

Rogers, E. M. (2003). *Diffusion of innovations, 5th Ed.* New York: Free Press.

Rogers, E. M. (2004). A prospective and retrospective look at the diffusion model. *Journal of Health Communication*, 9:13-19.

Rossi, P. H., Lipsey, M. W., & Freeman, H. E. (2004). *Evaluation: A systematic approach, 7th Ed.* Thousand Oaks, CA: Sage Publications, Inc.

Schrage, M. (2004). Innovation diffusion. *Technology Review*, 107:10.

Shapiro, S. P. (1990). Collaring the crime, not the criminal: Reconsidering the concept of white-collar crime. *American Sociological Review*, 55:346-355.

Shaw, C. R., & McKay, H. D. (1942). *Juvenile delinquency and urban areas*. Chicago: University of Chicago Press.

Shover, N., & Hochsteller, A. (2006). *Choosing white-collar crime*. New York: Cambridge University Press.

Shover, N. & Wright, J. P. (Eds.) (2001). *Crimes of privilege: Readings in white-collar crime*. New York: Oxford University Press.

Smith, B. C. (2007). The subprime mortgage market, a review and compilation of research and commentary. October 19, 2007. The Homer Hoyt Institute.

Snyder, P. J., Priem, R. L., & Levitas, E. (2009). The diffusion of illegal innovations among management elites. Paper presentation at the *Annual Meeting of the Academy of Management*, Chicago, 2009.

Stiglitz, J. E. (2008). It doesn't take Nostradamus. *Economist's Voice*, November, 2008. Berkeley Electronic Press.

Strang, D., & Soule, S. A. (1998). Diffusion in organizations and social movements: From hybrid corn to poison pills. *Annual Review of Sociology*, 24:265-290.

Sutherland, E. H. (1940). White-collar criminality. *American Sociological Review*, 5:1-12.

Sutherland, E. H. (1983). *White-collar crime: The uncut version*. London: Yale University Press.

Sykes, G. M., & Matza, D. (1957). Techniques of neutralization: A theory of delinquency. *American Sociological Review*, 22:664-670.

Tittle, C. R., Burke, M. J., & Jackson, E. F. (1986). Modeling Sutherland's theory of differential association: Toward an empirical clarification. *Social Forces*, 65:405-432.

Trajtenberg, M. & Yitzhaki. (1989). The diffusion of innovations: A methodological reappraisal. *Journal of Business & Economic Statistics*, 7:35-47.

United States Securities and Exchange Commission (SEC) (2010). Available at http://www.sec.gov/. Last visited on January 9, 2010.

United States Securities and Exchange Commission (SEC) (2012). Available at http://www.sec.gov/. Last visited on March 24, 2012.

Utt, R. D. (2008). Subprime mortgage problems: A quick tour through the rubble. *WebMemo No. 1881*. Heritage Foundation. Retrieved on October 15, 2009 from: www.heritage.org/Research/Economy/wm1881.cjm.

Valente, T. W. (2005). Network models and methods for studying the diffusion of innovations. In Peter J. Carrington, John Scott, and Stanley Wasserman (Eds.), *Models and Methods in Social Network Analysis*, (pp. 98-116). New York: Cambridge University Press.

Weisburd, D., Wyckoff, L. A., Ready, J., Eck, J. E., Hinkle, J. C., & Gajewski, F. (2006). Does crime just move around the corner? A controlled study of spatial displacement and diffusion of crime control benefits. *Criminology*, 44:549-592.

Weiss, A. (1997). The communication of innovation in American policing. *Policing: An International Journal of Police Strategies & Management*, 20:292-310.

Westphal, J. D., Gulati, R., & Shortell, S. M. (1997). Customization or conformity? An institutional and network perspective on the content and consequences of TQM adoptions. *Administrative Science Quarterly*, 42: 366-394.

Whitworth, A. (2008). High rates of foreclosures lead to crime increases nationwide. *Geography & Public Safety*, 1:17-18.

Wilson, R. E., & Paulson, D. J. (2008). Foreclosures and crime: A geographical perspective. *Geography & Public Safety*, 1:1-2.

Zyglidopoulos, S. C., Fleming, P. J., & Rothenberg, S. (2008). Rationalization, overcompensation and the escalation of corruption in organizations. *Journal of Business Ethics*, 84:65-73.

Index